The Corporate Zone

The Corporate Zone

David S. Olson

iUniverse, Inc.
New York Lincoln Shanghai

The Corporate Zone

Copyright © 2005 by David Olson

iUniverse books may be ordered through booksellers or by contacting:

iUniverse
2021 Pine Lake Road, Suite 100
Lincoln, NE 68512
www.iuniverse.com
1-800-Authors (1-800-288-4677)

ISBN-13: 978-0-595-37367-3 (pbk)
ISBN-13: 978-0-595-81764-1 (ebk)
ISBN-10: 0-595-37367-4 (pbk)
ISBN-10: 0-595-81764-5 (ebk)

Printed in the United States of America

This book is dedicated to my parents, family and friends who have encouraged me to pursue this endeavor until completion. In the likely event that my current employment should cease shortly after the release of this manuscript, you all will be hearing from me in short order. I would also like to thank many co-workers who, over the years, have inadvertently provided more than enough material and inspiration. Also to MADDOG who, in his infinite wisdom, told me over a cocktail at a wonderful little outdoor bar on Grand Cayman Island, "They can kill you but they can't eat you."

Contents

Preface

So, you would like to be the CEO of a major corporation some day? Well I'm here to tell you that even when you make it you'll still have plenty of work and challenge cut out for you. Today's business climate is tough and getting tougher every day. With world-wide competition, an insatiable lust for performance on Wall Street, an incredibly diverse work force and technology advancements coming at a mind boggling pace, life at the top of the pyramid is no easy task. Within your organization, you'll have many looking for you to stumble so they can have the chance to eat your lunch. Outside of it, Corporate Raiders large and small will circle like sharks feeding on the sick and the weak. Daily tasks such as obtaining quality information will seem nearly impossible with layer upon layer of individuals not wanting you to "shoot the messenger" if the news is less than stellar. It may be a life long dream but rest assured it's lonely at the Top! Well don't worry, the benefits at the summit aren't too shabby either and well worth the struggle. The poor man wants to be rich and the rich man wants to be king. The corporate life is great because the sky is the limit; just don't let the bastards get you down, ever. The strong will survive. I've had the pleasure of working for some of the best companies in the world from start-ups to fortune 500 and they all have incredible challenges and fantastic rewards so please forgive me in advance for the cynical tone which may have a habit of permeating into the pages to follow. For me, it has been a great ride and I take great pride in the goods and services that are only available through the heroic efforts of corporate employees who reside at all levels of the pyramid. Anyway, you've got a lot to learn before you get the chance to show the world what you can do so let's get started and the very best place to start is at the bottom!

Intro

How many times have you stopped to reflect, with the thought in mind, if I only knew then what I know now, how much better your life might have been? Well, by reading this book, you can avoid future reflections and ensure that your career dreams come true. Or perhaps you'll decide to reconsider what those dreams really ought to be.

The following pages will reveal how ordinary people can make astounding accomplishments. People who, by luck and experience, have managed to achieve success without compromising who they are. This may sound very natural and straightforward but it's not that simple in reality. I once asked an executive, of a fortune 100 company, how an employee could bring a new idea to fruition in his organization. He stated that it was rather easy to start a "grass roots" type of movement and then things would "kind of" take care of themselves. Since, at the time, I was the employee with an idea to promote, I can honestly tell you it goes a little more like this. Pretend for a minute that you are a salmon. The biggest, strongest salmon that there ever was. Your journey up the river to accomplish your mission will tire you and eventually leave you dead. So please enjoy the swim along the way.

The concepts presented hereafter will not likely be taught in any classroom but they will help illustrate some of the little dramas that are played out in every business, every day of the week, all over the world.

Don't be offended by the brutal honesty that is inevitable when describing human behavior and keep an open mind knowing that what you stand to gain is knowledge that could otherwise take you many years to attain on your own. The chapters that follow carry funny little titles to help you appreciate the progress you'll be making in awareness of the "not so obvious". Be assured, the conditioning you will receive will help you to embrace unwanted sarcasm and endless roadblocks with open arms and a smile on your face.

1

Corporations—The Great "Legalized" Pyramids

Welcome. You're about to enter The Corporate Zone. A place like no other on earth with mysteries unimaginable to those who have not yet entered the iron gates. Your innocence of youth, education, religion and family upbringing are about to be shattered like a giant pane of glass.

But do not fear. There is a way, a way to survive, a way to thrive and with a tremendous amount of luck, maybe even a way to preserve your sanity. Never let anyone get the better of you because they're sure going to try. One of my all time favorite lines, from the movie Point of No Return, is spoken by Bridget Fonda after her character witnesses a brutal murder. She simply looks up at the man who committed the crime and smiles and says, "I never did mind about the little things." This little line keeps her alive in the movie and it will help keep you alive too if you remember it and use it when you're in those tough "little" situations. I am not suggesting that you will be a witness to murder in your place of business but it is quite likely that you will witness several things just as shocking.

Why is it that the old moneymaking pyramid scams are illegal yet corporate executives are thriving on much the same principle?

If you go to work, as I did, for one of those mega companies, with say over 30,000 employees, consider how many of those people will have the responsibility of supervising other employees. If each person in a supervisory role has 10 people reporting to him or her, it could work out to over 3000. That's a lot of people that are solely charged with looking after others. Now you may get lucky and find a few coaches and mentors among them, but more then likely the majority will be highly focused only on what's good for them. If you think, "that's OK,

I'll meet lots of friends and coworkers who will help me along", think again. Your colleagues, by design, will need to become your competition if they are to ever separate themselves from the crowd in order to ascend to the higher levels of the pyramid. In many ways, you'll find out that you're on your own.

2

Getting Started—"The Idiot Stage."

Congratulations, you've just landed your first position! Filled with all of the excitement and energy of a 6-month-old Labrador retriever puppy, you prepare for that glorious first day. New clothes, hair, optimism and Franklin Planner in hand, you begin your journey. Remember to drive carefully as one of you rear-ended my truck at a stoplight one day! Relax, the first week may be a little nerve wracking, but this is your only chance to make a good first impression. After the formalities of filling the benefits forms out, you'll be shown your cubicle (hereafter referred to as the burlap kennel) and be introduced to about a thousand people in a very scientific sequence. The people in the department where you'll be working come first, followed by anyone that you run into that the person escorting you recognizes. A designee and never a real boss will perform this task. Smile, be polite and socialize to the best of your ability. Don't worry about impressing your supervisor this week, as they will undoubtedly be on vacation or at some kind of bogus seminar. During any idle time that will invariably come up, jot down a few notes on who's who so that during the second week when a complete stranger starts talking to you like a long lost friend, you may recall which one of the thousand people this wacko is!

OK—several days have gone by and now you know where the restrooms and cafeteria are located and if you're an over achiever, you'll even remember the correct address to put on your business card order form. What, did you think that there would be an administrative assistant for taking care of that type of trivial task? Sorry, they're gone with the dinosaurs. Or if they do exist in your new corporate realm, they will be far too important and "busy" to do jack for you. But be sure to get them a card on secretary's day anyway. This type of gesture is called "seed planting", a very important technique and practice is important. Seed planting

3

should not be confused with brown-nosing as it can be done regardless of rank. There are several different types of seed planting and sometimes the results are positive and sometimes they're not. We'll talk about this technique in more detail later on.

It's week three, Monday morning and as you approach the front entrance suddenly you realize that you've forgotten your ID badge. The scowl you see on the face of the half asleep security guard makes you feel like a complete idiot. At this moment, it may be hard to even remember your own name as you fill out the paper temporary pass that was designed to call attention to the negligence of you—the "new" guy. Don't fret, this feeling will soon pass, the fact that you are indeed an idiot will take much longer to overcome. You have a B.S. in Mechanical Engineering and a M.B.A. you say? Well Ok, but only idiots wear the temporary badge and yours is on isn't it? Just try to keep a low profile and remind yourself that it happens to everybody sooner or later.

The early weeks are a great time to start getting a jump on your competition. You remember, the other idiots who went through orientation with you. Be aware of the fact that they are not new co-workers and colleagues; they're actually future adversaries who, sooner or later, will desperately want to see you screw up. Because if that happens, they'll have a better chance of surviving that "infant mortality" phase. You didn't forget about natural selection already did you? Anyway, a good way to start gaining your competitive edge is by developing a personal company acronym list. This list will eventually help you to decipher the secret language spoken by all those "in the know." Without a thorough knowledge of this foreign language, you will remain a stranger in a strange land. Corporate Executives can form complete sentences using only acronyms and they will talk this way around you because you're a new idiot and therefore present an irritation for them. Keep your list, like a closely guarded secret, as you will have to work hard to develop it on your own. Never, ever let anyone see that you have such a list because you'll want to listen to as many conversations as you can while people still think you're clueless. It's a good idea to ask what one of the languageless words means from time to time even though you already know the answer. Instead of using any of these sacred words at this stage, demonstrate your knowledge in non-threatening ways by suggesting good restaurants, movies or talk trivia about your geographical area. Work relatively long hours for the next three months. Obviously you won't really have anything to do yet, but it will validate your, soon to be used, first little white lie. At the very first opportunity, when asked by someone of your same level how it's going, tell him or her "I'm so busy." Of course you'll know that it's just from basic training sessions and talking to friends on the phone but they won't. You never know who's listening and it's important to always be busy. Now is a very good time to start boning up on those local restaurants. Also, spend hard time mastering every option of the voice messaging system, E-mail and E-calendars. Find out how to send voice messages directly into other's voice mail rather then actually having to talk to someone you don't like. Turn your computer on and off automatically but disarm this feature if it is known you will not be in the office for the day. Do a good job on the trivial tasks that start coming your way. Be prompt, polite and don't overdo the "busy" thing. Don't be too busy for your supervisor or other management either. That will come later. Since this is a job, many tasks will seem less than appealing. Find out early which ones you enjoy and excel at those. That way, the lesser tasks will start gravitating toward the other idiots. Be very visible when you come in early or stay late. But keep a low profile if you need to be away for more important personal business. Bringing in an occasional treat for the group is a very good idea, but don't do it often, on the same day of the week, or have it tied to any external occasion. Don't be predictable and don't wait on anyone, simply set them out in a common area to be enjoyed. As the new kid on the block, expect the extra duties like being assigned to the company picnic committee. This will be irritating because it will distract you from making a good impression or temporarily ruin your focus on the idiot competition, but try to have some fun with it. Network with the talkative employees who have been around a while rather then applying yourself to the crappy assignment. Soon enough you will learn to master the fine art of avoiding delegation. Start getting to know the people who really run the organization. You'll find that the real decision makers comprise less then ten percent of the actual population. Most of the other idiots occupy positions that are so task oriented that they are almost completely interchangeable from one company to another. Be friendly to everyone at your workplace but try very hard to keep your "real friends" outside of the office. These are the only people you can truly choose to remain as your friends, or not, depending on the circumstances. Maintaining a network of friends outside the workplace is truly important.

Whenever possible, start avoiding director level people that use the word "fun" too often in the workplace for they have forgotten the true meaning of the word long ago. Work hard for those who have a reputation for proper project assignments as well as supporting others. If one gives you a challenge, they are showing faith in your abilities. Organizational charts may be of some help during this whole "getting to know you" phase if someone can find you one. Be mindful of the fact that it will be out of date if you do get one. If you still have idle time, take a look at the policy book. Don't stress out if you can't make heads or tails of it. More importantly, find out what the unwritten policies are from savvy peers.

3

Image is everything. Graduating from an Idiot to a "Jib."

Do you believe that all people are created equally? If you do great, but surely you will agree that they are not created the same. There are infinite combinations of physical features alone. Now add the knowledge and values learned through education and years of experience you acquired growing up and wow. This will make the task of separating yourself from the other idiots very complicated. What does any of this have to do with your future career you might be asking yourself? Well, everything. Consider this, if you were a talented young athlete or an extremely attractive person who also happens to be lucky enough to be photogenic, would you be reading this book? No. You are among the majority forced to work for a living in positions that, at the end of the day, you can hopefully be proud of. In order to stand out, in a good way, you will want to have your image work for you rather than against you. Don't worry; this can be accomplished without totally sacrificing any of the outlandish things you may enjoy doing. For example, many executives ride Harley Davidson motorcycles on the weekends but very few will appear in the boardroom with their leathers on! Since you will be working with and for other people, it is inevitable that you will be stereotyped. Even most movie stars seem to get typecast after a very short time. Think about the image you want others to see when they look at you. The part of your personality that is expressed by your exterior appearance is very important in the business world. If you wear something revealing to a nightclub when out with your friends and a coworker happens to run into you, you've suddenly become more intriguing. Wear the same outfit to the company holiday party, just once, and you'll attain a totally different stigma. This doesn't mean you can't show a little sex appeal. By all means if you've got it, flaunt it. But if done subtly, you'll maximize the positive impact and minimize the glares. Always be mindful of geographical norms for dress. On a recent business trip to Puerto Rico, where the dresses are low cut and tend to be very short in length, someone in Personnel approached a coworker of mine. It seems that there had been a complaint about the fact that she was wearing shorts in the office. It didn't matter that it was 95 degrees outside or that her tasteful white shorts were at least 6 inches longer then most of the skirts being worn that day. She was wearing shorts when appropriate dress required slacks or a skirt. It was easy to come up with a new nickname for her after that day. Don't kid yourself; they will have secret little nicknames for you too. Just don't make it easy on them to create derogatory ones that may last. Speaking of nicknames, your main goal at this point is to graduate from an idiot to a jib. Therefore, it's a good time to start taking some in depth observations of other jibs. Although some of my friends love to use this word, I have never heard a good definition for "jib" but I think you'll get the picture soon enough. Here is a little clue. One sure sign that you are becoming a jib is when you start dressing in company logo-wear on a regular basis. Being a jib is a good thing and most of us will always have some jib-like qualities.

4

Observing other Jibs in the "Work Place."

The following individuals and employee groups have been observed, stereotyped and documented to help you get started with jib identification and classification. Many of the people you meet will fall into one or more of these categories. It is important to remember that companies aren't bad. It's the people the work there that can drive you crazy!

The Golden Retriever (I told you there would be nicknames)

There is no dog more intelligent or faithful then the golden retriever. My first dog was a golden and I was totally impressed with him from the day I brought him home. Before getting the time to build a proper kennel, the dog spent a few days sleeping in my garage. Having bought a book on dog training, I figured it was time to start with the basics. The first time he made a small lake in the middle of the floor, I quickly got some newspaper and soaked up the mess making sure that the pup was watching my every move. After that was done, I put another section of the paper in the corner of the garage and had him come over to sniff it. I was hoping he made an association and would pee on top of the paper the next time he got the urge. A little while later, I returned to visit the pup. When I did, he walked to the middle of the garage and created another puddle. Just when I thought he hadn't got the message at all, he ran over to the corner, grabbed the paper in his little mouth and proceeded to lay the paper right on top of the wet spot. Golden retrievers are easy to spot in the work place. They are the loyal ones who have been around for years, built the company up and have only asked for a few pats along the way in return. Being one of these goldens is a great thing, in fact if not for them, the rest of the jibs probably would never make it. If you plan to aspire to the level of a golden retriever, you will enjoy reading about the rest of these characters, as it will give you extra pride in your chosen style!

Hockey Dads

Working full time while having four kids playing ice hockey is an incredibly difficult challenge. The people who schedule ice time pick the most inconvenient hours possible for games and practice. I have witnessed two distinctly different hockey dads in action. One was determined to climb the corporate ladder (and he did) while the other was perfectly happy seeing his kids advance in the sport and work was something that merely killed time between games. The thing about hockey dads is that, no matter what their career ambition is, all they talk about is hockey. I seriously wonder what these guys would do if challenged to not watch, talk about, coach or otherwise have any association with the game for just one week out of their lives. I don't think some of them could do it. Why pick on hockey dads? Well if you end up working with or for one of these guys, I sure hope you love the game. If you don't, all I can say is good luck trying to relate! Besides, we are going to pick on everyone sooner or later.

Presentation Paula

It's very common to be asked to give a presentation shortly after being hired for a large company. There are many reasons this is done. It gives management a good opportunity to see who of the new recruits has the confidence and other skills required to speak to groups of people. It also provides for a full time slot on their calendars ensuring they won't need to perform any tasks that would require some intense level of thought. Beware of Presentation Paula during this period. If you give a mediocre presentation and you're followed by Paula, you're in for big trouble. You see, Paula lives to create and give the perfect presentation. It's not that she is extremely bright or that she has something that important to say, but this is her thing. She knows nothing about the game of hockey and has no interest in doing anything besides presenting boring material. In this day of computerized showmanship, even Paula can dazzle a zombie-like crowd given she has brought adequate treats and a killer Power Point presentation. Were you thinking you were going to get away with a joke and a couple of overheads? Paula is smiling at you already knowing that you're still an idiot or at best a fumbling jib. No doubt Paula will be striving for an Academy Award with her multimedia glitz. Remember, this is a competitive time and you will lose this round to Paula every time and that's OK because, after all, no one is really listening anyway.

Fast Fred

Fred is among the slowest walkers on the face of the earth. Given this, Fred will always gravitate to a position that requires a fair amount of foot travel during the course of his day. You may find it necessary to line Fred up with an inanimate object just to get a read on whether he is in fact moving or not. Fred is a friendly guy but try to visit him while he is sitting, as you will find it virtually impossible to slow down to his speed in order to have a walking conversation.

Competitive Carla

The study of others is very important as it helps us to define the qualities we want to project in our own lives. Carla has no need to study others because, quite frankly, she is better at everything already. Carla is intensely competitive in all that she does.

The Artful Dodger

Art loves "working" for the company. He'll be among the employees that are perpetually smiling. Art loves everything about everything. He thinks we have the best management team and the greatest mission statement ever created. Art survives entirely on positive energy. But take a closer look at Art's behavior and you'll realize that he is so busy being positive that he doesn't really get anything accomplished. Art has sharply developed the skills necessary to avoid any delegation. He can dodge more bullets then Keanu Reeves' character in the movie, The Matrix. But go ahead and ask him if he's busy and my money will be on his affirmative response. Art floats through life much the same way in which water moves on earth. Under the force of gravity, it flows to reach its own level. In order to accomplish this, it will take the easiest possible path and then rest there indefinitely. It takes a major force of nature to upset this resting condition so that it will, once again, flow. Art will be among the last employees to show up in the morning and definitely among the first to go home. If Art happens to be a Hockey Dad as well, no one will question his attendance because who could fault Art for being so attentive of his children by attending all of their games? During the few hours while actually residing in his burlap kennel, you will likely find Art killing time by shooting the breeze with old college hockey buddies or arranging the next banquet.

Edina Ellie

In the state where I grew up, there is an affluent little town called Edina. Edina, it turns out, is really an acronym for Every Day I Need Attention. Ellie grew up in Edina. Ellie is Edina personified. She was the prettiest little cheerleader and homecoming queen you ever saw. Popularity is the name of Ellie's game. You can bet that the conversation always centers on Ellie when she is around. Ellie gets by on good looks and a bubbly personality. The fashion industry is the only benefactor of Ellie's paycheck. In fact, the term "High Maintenance" was coined with Ellie in mind. The only crisis in Ellie's life will stem from a bad hair day. Ellie will quickly demonstrate her incompetence because, for Ellie, job performance is of no concern. Why should it be, she relied on her boyfriends to get her through school, why change now! Good looks alone will ensure Ellie survives the strongest of storms. Ellie will not and cannot report to any female supervisors. If by some twist of fate this were to happen, Ellie would seek an immediate transfer to once again ensure her prosperity. Other then the occasional good office party, Ellie thrives on boondoggles, leaves of absence, and worthless training sessions. Yes Ellie is tall, beautiful and has perfect hair. Other female employees, serious about their careers, never befriend Ellie.

Finance Frank

The most interesting thing about Frank is that he doesn't really even know what his company manufactures. He has never taken a walk on the production floor. This is mainly because Frank is under the illusion that he's in upper management, when, after all, he has no functional authority. Frank is merely a Monday morning quarterback in nice clothes and he's anxious to give you a very lengthy play by play of the recent bottom line figures. For Frank, it's all about the numbers. Quarterly reports are his specialty. You know how a great comedian can find such funny subject matter in observing every day events? Well Frank achieves the opposite. He can take a subject that everyone is keenly interested in and make it as boring as watching grass grow. As he presents the first slide, you'll have all of the anticipation of a child at Christmas time. But within only a few minutes Frank will completely lose you. After a few more minutes, audible groans will be heard as everyone clears their throat and adjusts their chairs in a feeble attempt to stay awake. Frank will be oblivious to the impatience; he is just warming up for his next thirty slides. Where is Presentation Paula when you need her? Frank will always have too many ways to look at the same information and this should not be a big surprise, as what else has he got to do until the next quarterly meeting? Don't expect any treats from Frank as his passion is pinching those pennies not spending them on you. At the end of Frank's painful dissertation, the "senior" management present will give much kudos to him. This comes as if Frank had anything to do with whatever success may have been realized!

Humane Resources

In my experience, the folks in the Human Resources Department are among the nicest people that you will ever meet. Chat with them and enjoy their company but remember one little fact. They only have two real responsibilities in their career, to hire and grow new employees and to kiss up to management. Don't expect them to do any of the traditional HR tasks as you will now personally complete any necessary paper work, etc., normally associated with this function, at your desk via some overpriced software package. It is ironic that there is so much automation in an area of the organization that should be people friendly. A current colleague told me about an experience he had while researching the job opportunities at an excellent large local organization. As the story goes, he had gone on line to view advanced engineering listings. The software this company used prompted him to input his interests and qualifications. He said that very quickly a position was highlighted as a "best fit". After a short time of reviewing the job description, he realized this was a position he was very interested in. When prompted, he clicked the button to apply. He went on to say that in merely seconds he received a response saying that he was under qualified for this position. Their loss turned out to be our gain!

One of the things that irritates me the most is when employees are referred to merely as "head count" by a representative of Management or Human Resources Department. This is a common term sanctioned by HR departments, but I personally can't think of a more dehumanizing term coming from a group that professes to be interested in personnel development.

The "Diversity" Department

This relatively newly created department has been given the titanic sized responsibility of training away our lifelong prejudice. I use the term titanic as my first awareness of this department came when ours hit a little bit of an iceberg. For weeks, they had been planning for a day of celebrating diversity. The excitement must have been running high because there was much fanfare and several reminders via email. However, when the big day arrived, a cancellation notice was sent out. It seems they overlooked the fact that this was the first day of Rosh Hashanah! No doubt that after that oversight, they let several months go by while keeping a pretty low profile. But when that incident blew over, they came back stronger then ever. It seems that diversity had become the topic of a recent best seller and therefore a priority. A three-day intensive brainwashing session was to be given to every employee and of course it had the support of top management! Most everyone I know would have chosen dancing on red-hot coals over this experience. But unfortunately, attendance was mandatory and the signatures on the training records were not solicited until the end of each session. Some things will be unavoidable, so take a deep breath and get them over with. Can't wait to see what comes next from this ridiculous group!

Engineers

Engineers rarely smile. Growing up with more brains than social does that to a person. But don't fret if you're an engineer, you can learn how to smile. Did you ever notice how many people try to play engineer? Heck, they even started adding "Engineer" to the end of such prefixes as "Sanitation". Be proud of what you do because no one else will even understand what the hell you're talking about if you try to explain what you do!

The Instant Expert

Let's call this guy Ed the Expert. Ed will drive you insane. Ed is the type of guy who can listen to something once and repeat it verbatim. He is so skilled at this technique that his career will soar. It doesn't matter if Ed has half of the intelligence of any other peer, he totally sounds like an expert. Ed will rely heavily on work done by others but he will never stoop so low as to give anyone else an ounce of credit. If you have an Ed in upper management, you can expect that your entire organization will march to the beat of the last book that Ed read. If you happen to have an Ed sitting in the adjacent burlap kennel, you're screwed.

The only thing that could be worse would be if he were also related to the top honcho. Instant Experts are highly confident people but they are never well liked!

Trudy the Idea Thief

On the outside, Trudy appears to be a very introspective person. She listens very carefully as people discuss their days and ideas around the water coolers. Whenever someone actually makes a significant statement, something very odd happens physically to Trudy. First her head turns slightly away from the crowd. After a slight delay, the rest of her body will follow is if being pulled through her neck. As her right hand rises slowly to meet her chin, her head will simultaneously cant downward approximately 10 degrees or so. It appears that Trudy has removed herself for a moment of deep thought, which indeed she has. Her mind is racing because she needs to figure out how to spin the idea she just heard into her own. She will need to move quickly and precisely to capitalize on this little beauty before anyone else does. A slight smile comes across Trudy's face as her posture returns to that of one of the "rest of the gang". The whole act was just to try and convey that she didn't really hear what was just said. Now she's armed and needs to find just the perfect target to maximize the "suck up" potential of the moment. Being the artist that she is, Trudy finds a way to strike quickly in such a way that the damage won't be revealed for some time. By the time it is, history will be written.

Squirrel in the Road

This one should be self-explanatory. If you see an employee acting as confused as a "squirrel in the middle of the road", run over them and don't look back!

The Yes Man

For the life of me, I do not understand these people. What tragic event happened to them at a younger age to result in such pathetic creatures? It's not that they lack intelligence; it's just that any modicum of courage was surgically removed long ago. They are close relatives of the "Squirrel in the Road" folks and will be run over as well.

Johnny the Invisible Man

What kind of adult still prefers Johnny to John? Well it doesn't matter that much as this Johnny is truly invisible. He spends his day apologizing, moving out of the way and thinking about Ellie who, of course, won't give Johnny the time of day. Oh well, I guess the Johnny thing worked out for Mr. Carson on the Tonight Show. Take a look around, anyone named "Johnny" on your board?

Tangent Tom

I once had an individual reporting to me who turned out to be some kind of an expert on wood ticks. I didn't realize this fascinating tidbit until one day I heard him tell a colleague that there were several different types of wood ticks. I thought this was kind of interesting but continued on about my business. As I made a second pass through the hallway, nearly an hour and a half later, he was still talking about wood ticks. Although I always admire someone with fantastic memory retention for details, this was a bit much. Even more disturbing, was the fact that the other guy was still actively listening to this crap. When it gets right down to it, Tangent Toms just like the spotlight on them no matter what the subject matter is.

"By the Book" Bob

Bob was born with horse blinders permanently affixed to his head. If anything is done that is not exactly to company policy, Bob will be right there to let you know about it. Everybody's been told, growing up, that patience is a virtue. But if you have a few Bobs to hurdle on a daily basis, you will understand the full meaning of the phrase. Invariably, you will encounter two or three Bobs when in the position of having to prepare any written assignment that requires multiple signatures. Be prepared for the following sequence of events because it never changes. First, you will work your ass off creating a wonderful document. You'll look at all the options and consider the best approach to accomplish your goals. Then you'll type it up in a nice little format using your favorite font. All is great until you bring it to Bob #1 for sign off. Upon receipt, Bob will take several minutes of your time to inform you of just how busy he is but that he'll try to get to your work ASAP. At this point your pride and joy will get tossed on top of a huge pile of other lonely looking manuscripts created by countless other jibs and idiots. You walk away feeling good though because yours is on the "top" of the pile. By the time you return to your kennel, you'll start getting the uneasy feeling that maybe Bob has already rearranged the pile and of course he has! Approximately two to three weeks later, Bob will come around with something that once looked familiar but now seems to be hiding behind a tremendous amount of red ink chicken scratches. Bob will bring it to you personally to reemphasize just how important he is and to inform you that you used the incorrect font. What the hell were you thinking? A closer examination of the red ink will reveal that Bob has merely made a weak attempt at wordsmithing your masterpiece. He clearly does not have a clue of what you're trying to accomplish, he only cares about how powerful he feels by being the "sign off" guy. At this point you can try using reason with Bob to see if he'll ignore the changes and just sign the damn thing. But if you do, you will only heighten the sense of frustration that is starting to swell up inside of you like an ocean tide. So after beating your head against the wall several times, you make Bob's changes and finally get his signature. Just when you feel like popping the cork on a cheap bottle of champagne, you're informed that Bob #2 needs to review and sign off on your document also. The process starts all over again. The difference between being an idiot or a jib is huge in this situation, as the savvier jib will perform this task in parallel rather then in serial. A real seasoned jib may even insight a Bob fight over some obscure policy just for entertainment. The main area you will find a high concentration of Bobs is in the Quality Department of any organization you may happen to visit.

Consultant Chris

Chris is no high-test fast performer by any stretch of the imagination. You see, consultants are paid by the hour and being to the point and efficient would be, by design, counterproductive to Chris's paycheck. Chris is a master of PC solitaire. The beauty of Chris's MO is that nobody seems to notice or even care that he spends endless hours playing the game. I'm not sure whether Chris ever wins at the damn thing, but what does he care anyway? Don't get me wrong Chris is very intelligent. It takes a pretty smooth operator to get paid this much for doing so little. Seek out Chris in your workplace, as you will find him full of great advice on just about anything you can imagine. By the way, he will have plenty of time to tell you all about whatever you want to know. The thing you will come to realize, and this is excruciatingly frustrating, is the fact that the only reason management hired Chris in the first place is that they refused to listen to their own people. I can guarantee that whatever project Chris gets assigned to would have been handled ten times better by someone already there, and at a fraction of the cost.

Big Word Betty

What planet did Betty grow up on? She uses words that no one has ever heard in virtually every sentence she speaks. Her intent is to impress everyone with her vast knowledge but the result is that nobody will talk to her because they don't have a clue as to what she is trying to say. You may come across Betty having a conversation with herself, as she is the only one worthy of challenge in vocabulary. Betty, more than likely, is a chemist.

Anxious Al

Al's got problems. If you ask him "how's it going?" you're likely to hear about his bad stomach, sore neck or any one of a multitude of other maladies. People learn quickly to avoid this greeting when encountering Al. Any ambiguous business situation will cause Al tremendous amounts of anxiety. A pending organization change, which may include Al's department, is cause for great concern. You may find that Al's hands actually shake during these periods of uncertainty. Al will not be among the big risk takers of the organization and as a result will experience little upward movement. Al is a good guy to chat with occasionally, as he will always have his radar up looking for something to worry about. Most people are somewhat resistant to change, some people embrace it, but Al deathly fears it.

Candace the Critic

Candace doesn't like anything or anybody. She has a major chip on her shoulder because they just don't appreciate her genius. She will spend her days creating little conspiracy theories, most of which will hit the nail right on the head. Candace will continue down a path of alienation that will last for the rest of her career. She will only have friends that tend to be just like her.

Marketing Folks

Marketing people are very lucky indeed. It seems that they always have the biggest budget and the most fun. This is the only department where you are likely to find a predominance of relatively creative people. However, they often are as confused about being part of the management team as the finance folks. During the holidays, their burlap kennels will be decorated with lively little trinkets that were placed with the greatest of care. I have always thought it would be great to work there. Wouldn't an advertising company be a blast to work for? I heard of one that was so in tune with keeping their people creative that if they lost a bid, on a big ad campaign, that they would throw a party so that no one would dwell on the current failure. You won't hear about this happening in too many departments in your new company!

Sales

Everyone has seen the ads that go like this, "The Few, the Proud, the Marines." Corporate sales people must get the exact same training as Marines when they hire on. They will posses all of the social graces that the Engineers lack. They will take no prisoners in their attempt to break all previous sales goals. They are quite personable, but never to be trusted. They are, however, necessary evils. Or are they? I always thought a great product should be able to sell itself. Oh well, we still need someone to take those buyers out to dinner.

Buyers

Buyers love being catered to by sales representatives. Although they pretend to be tough negotiators, it's really all about the perks for them. You don't need to pay these guys too much as they could damn near live off of their perks. Like sales people, buyers are well versed in all things athletic. They don't hang around the kennel too much because their office is the golf course, fishing boat, or some lavish retreat. By the way, they do pay for all the perks through inflated prices, but they won't care because they don't get paid crap!

"Senior Titles"

Man do people get hung up on titles! What is the big deal about a stinking label? I guess everybody wants the respect they feel they've earned, but is this the best way we have to convey our countless hours of blood, sweat and tears? Most perplexing to me is the "senior" title e.g. "Senior Accountant". I just can't figure out if these people are old or if they have just been doing the same thing for far too long. Sorry all you Golden Retrievers out there but you know I love you! The intent of this title is obvious; a strong experienced performer who is given more responsibility. Often times, it is desired that they direct or mentor other junior level peers. At least, this is what the definition says somewhere in a HR document. The sad thing is that, all too often, these Goldens are taken for granted on a daily basis. If they weren't, we sure wouldn't need any damn consultants. If you ask a "Senior" what extra authority or resources they have been given in order to perform at these higher expectations, they will look more perplexed then any real golden retriever that has lost a bone. Can't get that image of a white faced dog out of my mind when I think about people with "Senior" titles.

5

Pastimes of the Office

Now that you have spent a little time observing the jibs, why not find a few new ways to kill some idle time. It more then likely will take several more weeks before you get busy with anything too intense. The following is only a partial list, but it should be enough to help get your own creative thoughts going:

Browsing for Brownies

This technique is one that is very easy to learn. Quite simply, when you feel like avoiding any real work, start walking the halls looking for any treats that have been left out. This can be a long process or a short one based on your needs. The main thing to remember, while browsing for brownies, is that you must always carry a notebook or file so that it will appear as if you're actually working. Look around your office and you may be surprised at just how much time the Tangent Toms spend doing this.

Coffee Breaks

Making several trips to the coffee pot or water cooler will provide nice short breaks from the daily grind. This is the most common and highly accepted method of catching up on a little gossip. If you practice this pastime often, it will be inevitable that the coffee pot will be empty from time to time and someone will need to make a fresh pot. Unless you have been seen approaching and have no other choice, don't do it. People who perform this type of trivial task will be labeled as "Coffee Makers" and will not climb the ladder. Just take a glass of water quickly instead and pretend you're in too big of a hurry to spend the 30 seconds it takes to make a fresh pot.

Potty time

The first boss I ever had was a terrific guy but he enjoyed a very strange office pastime. Every morning after his coffee he would quietly disappear into the bathroom for several hours. I was really feeling sorry for the guy, because what kind of gastrointestinal disease did he have? Well, we came to find out that he was just doing the crossword puzzle from the daily newspaper while sitting in the stall. He must have really loved them to go to that extreme in order to get the time to work on them!

Personal Computers, Games and the Internet

I have witnessed many people training for, what must be, the World Computer Solitaire Marathon Championships. Admittedly, I do not care for the game but how can anyone play it for hours on end? This is a mindless approach to devising an office pastime and I would recommend using those with a little more challenge or entertainment value. The Internet has become the most popular new pastime as it has something for everyone. Be very mindful of what is acceptable to others around you though. Sports, entertainment, Wall Street news, the Internet has it all. Sure, the damn thing is even good for legitimate research, but we are talking pastimes here. Use these computerized pastimes when people are less likely to be passing by your burlap kennel as they may pick up on a pattern of abuse.

The Boondoggle

A boondoggle is the gold standard of the office pastimes. They can come in the form of a training session, sales conference, quality audit or any one of several other categories. You need to learn all you can about positioning yourself to get included in the boondoggles that appeal to you. In addition to time away from the office, boondoggles provide the perfect method of accumulating frequent flyer miles, enjoying fine dining and top rate lodging. It can be difficult to break into the boondoggle club so pay close attention to those who are regularly on one.

The Great Escape of the Peon Level "My kids are sick"

This technique is the opposite of a boondoggle as there is no travel perks involved. It is amazing how healthy some employee's children are while others tend to have frequent minor maladies that require much parental attention. Today, companies are fairly good about allowing time for these situations, but invariably some employees will feel it is their duty to push this envelope as much as possible. I much prefer a boondoggle.

Do you Golf?

There has always been a lot of "business" done on golf courses. And given a choice between solitaire in a burlap kennel or golf on a beautiful course, it's an easy decision for me. If you don't play golf, learn! If you do not want to learn you must like solitaire or are just plain stubborn. Also learn the rules of "customer golf" and remember that the competition is between the golfer and the course not the person you're trying to make a sale to or get a raise from.

The Exercise Room

If you are lucky, your company will have a facility for exercising. Many people use these facilities every day for a much needed break as well as for the physical benefits. Exercise is always a good way to keep stress levels down. If you get into this habit, make sure you go during the morning or afternoon so as not to interfere with your lunch break!

Pencil Pushing

If you stayed up too late last night and you need a pastime that requires a little less energy, try something like this. Create a list of strange words that are only used in your office like:

Per
Scenario
Omnipresent
Paradigm
Ubiquitous

If you're really bored, you could have a little fun by modifying some of the acronyms from the list you've been compiling. For example:

C constantly

E evaluating
O options

M most
B boring
A acronym

P providing
E extra
R rewards to
K knuckleheads

You've got the idea. At least you'll look busy this way even if you're just pushing your pencil around!

Breaks for the Hourly

People in hourly positions hold their breaks as sacred time. Do not approach them during these fifteen minutes of bliss if you really need their help. They usually have a set time for their breaks and tend to not be very flexible if you show up during the middle of one. These folks aren't likely to be accomplished at browsing for brownies and they rarely get the chance to engage in a boondoggle, so this is their time to have coffee, look at the newspaper and relax. If you accidentally drop by during one, apologize for your negligence and come back later. Occasionally, hanging around and shooting the breeze can help you build rapport if the situation warrants. You will find that getting help from these groups is no problem after showing them a little respect for their down time.

6

The Environment

As you may have already observed, the environment in the typical office will most likely prove to be somewhat disappointing. Some buildings may have an impressive façade and a warm reception area but few will carry any sense of luxury into the trenches where the employees are housed. If you haven't paid close attention, it might be a good idea to get some practical expectations of the surroundings you're most likely to encounter.

Dimensions of the Burlap Kennel

Typically, the dimensions of your kennel will be tied to your position. For example, an engineer can expect an 8-foot by 8-foot home away from home. A manager may get an 8-foot by 12-foot and a technician may get stuck in a 6-foot by 8-foot. In some cases, two employees will get stuck in the same kennel for a period of time. Contemplating this provided me much irritation knowing that my golden retriever back home had a 6-foot by 12-foot kennel with a view! In fact in the summer time, he would even get a swimming pool to use as his pastime. Don't worry too much about kennel size because, contrary to popular belief, size will not matter when you're the master of boondoggles and browsing for brownies.

Cubicle Density & Noise

The modern day burlap kennel was designed to ensure that as many people as possible could be compressed into a given area. Since they are relatively easy to put up and to reconfigure, they offer a simple way to achieve flexibility without bringing in construction crews. However, they do very little in terms of privacy or morale. In a large area filled with hundreds of cubicles, it is amazing how many conversations can be heard simultaneously. If you have a talent for tuning out background noise you will have a huge advantage in cube land. It is important to remember though that at any given time several people will have the ability to hear every word you say. The wall height of the kennel also provides a problem, in that, if they are short you will feel rather exposed and if they are too tall you may begin to feel claustrophobic. All in all, burlap kennels provide a rather depressing place to spend time.

Lack of Inspirational Artwork

Management expectations are for you to be at your creative best. In order to help facilitate this, they will provide nothing on the walls of any aesthetic value. They will ensure there are no visual distractions, which might help clear the mind and actually inspire. Their thinking is that if you stare at a computer monitor for 8 hours a day that you will be productive. The only real result of this behavior is that CRT zombies are created. If you end up being close to a window, you will be lucky indeed. Any artwork you may see will no doubt be some old marketing poster or bogus SPC charting. Do your best to dress up your kennel a little bit. Bring in a colorful poster or some of your favorite pictures from your last vacation.

Poor Color Choice in Paint, Carpet and Tile

It's a sad statement when even "real men" start complaining about interior decorating. Where in the hell do they find the people that pick the colors for office buildings? Drab is the norm. We wouldn't want cheerful employees now would we? The carpet is also dull, and if it's not, it's because it was left over from the last local casino job. Any tile present will be arranged in a non-repeating pattern with colors that do not belong together.

Parking

In the long run, you can forget about using the fitness center. You will be parking so far away from your kennel that you won't need to go and work out. The distance from the front door will be proportional to the time you arrive, so get there early. But if you come in late, you may not even get a parking spot. However, try not to get upset if your boss has an assigned spot right up front next to the customer and visitor parking areas. You will notice that these reserved spaces will never be more than half full.

The Cafeteria

If you're lucky enough to have one, do not expect any fine dining. I think the concept is that if they're living in a kennel, we should feed them accordingly. However, you will come to appreciate this convenience on rainy or cold days. Besides, the best use of the cafeteria will be that it offers a good conference room when all of the normal ones are booked which will often be the case! If you're looking for a new pastime, go to the cafeteria and see how many idiots you can spot in a ten-minute period.

Office Machines

Has the vision of moving towards a paperless society made any progress? Has the computer really given us the power to put more leisure time back into our lives? Take a look around the office and you will see that printers and copiers seem to be the only mechanical devices that have truly advanced. We can copy, collate and staple at amazing speeds. Worthless email messages can be sent to hundreds of people with a mere click of the "send" button. How much of your life is now dedicated to sorting through junk mail? Is communication overload as bad as a lack of communication?

Kennel Maintenance

Although we examined several different jib personality traits earlier on, there are really only two kinds of jib when considering the care of their own personal kennel space. There is the neat jib and there is the stacker jib. The neat jib will have a place for everything and everything will be in its place. There will be a large percentage of visible desktop showing which of course will be dusted and cleaned on a regular basis. The neat jib will reserve a few minutes at the end of each week to ensure that there will be no clutter left in their area over the weekend. It's almost as if they expect some kind of inspection to occur while they are out.

The stacker jibs kennels will be quite the opposite. This is not to insinuate that the stacker will have any more difficulty in finding or retrieving any necessary documentation; it just means that you wouldn't have a prayer of finding anything in their domain. The stacker jib feels that it is their duty to retain anything and everything that crosses their desk. There will be no visible desktop space in these kennels as the stackers learn to work on top of the stacks that surround them and bring them such comfort. Some stacker's stacks even start at the floor level and ascend up to the desk and then from the desk on up. Accomplished stackers will pile as high as the kennel wall can provide support. Dust accumulation is definitely a problem for stackers as it is impossible to clean around all of that clutter. A stackers kennel may provide the illusion that this employee is "very busy" but a closer examination will reveal that the stacking process is a very gradual one. Although designated clean up and recycling days are targeted for the stackers, it will be only the neat jibs that actually participate. Moving days obviously are a source of much stress among the stacker crowd.

It can be very difficult to discern who is a neat jib and who is a stacker simply by just talking to and working with your colleagues. The only way to accurately resolve this fascinating mystery will be to go on a little walk-about to see who's who.

7

Thoughts on Behaviors related to "Classic Thinking."

Unfortunately, no one can provide you a detailed roadmap for success in the corporate world. Each one of us must find our own unique path by getting out in the world and trying our best to succeed with our given talents and intuitions. However, the following discussions should help you start to think about how to negotiate your own path.

Shaping Young Minds, the Traditional "Kissing Up" Approach

Most of us are told early in life that you will need to work hard in order to succeed in life. While this will always hold true, it doesn't begin to touch on the many other facets that need to compliment a strong work ethic. To further complicate this is the fact that every work environment will require different contributions. So what should you look for? Remember earlier that we talked about competition among peers? This is a good time to take a closer examination of what you can do, in addition to working hard and occasionally browse for a brownie, to stand out. You will, above all else, want to portrait yourself as a highly valuable employee. Do not set your sights on being the best at everything. This is simply not possible. Demonstrate your strengths and work hard to improve your areas of weakness. When you do reach the point where you become a recognized authority in a given area, never be pompous. Another difficult aspect of this phase will be knowing when to challenge convention. Some supervisors will welcome a confronting approach while others will have little or no tolerance for this. But remember that change is inevitable and without it continuous improvement will not be realized. Many companies rely too heavily on old established processes. Not that a proven process isn't necessary, it's that you also need a process to ensure your processes continually improve. Too many companies overlook this important concept. A small business owner once told me "People let the business run them rather then other way around!" Keep this in mind and look for ways you can make overall systemic improvements. When you find some, you certainly will differentiate yourself from the jib still making the coffee. You will witness other employees trying to impress people by using the old "kissing up" techniques. We all learned to do some kissing up when we were young because we were so eager to please. But in the office, you will want to show a more reserved and professional approach. One common kiss up method is when an employee tries to ask a significant question, usually during a large meeting, merely to sound impressive. You can be sure, eager employees like this will be called upon to do the little tasks.

True Genius, Where is the next Leonardo?

How many people do you know that can operate a television set? I would guess that your answer would be just about everyone you know including very young children. Now think about how many people you know who can fix a TV set? Finally, how many could design a better TV then anything on the market? Maybe you're not an electronics genius, but you do have a special area of expertise. Certainly people are born with genetic areas of strength, but true genius is learned only through years of great effort. Think about the millions of people in the world today who benefit from the work of a few individuals. If you study the contributions of just two, Thomas Edison and Leonardo da Vinci, you will be truly amazed. These are not the type of people who would have killed all of their time playing PC solitaire. That is, if it were available. These two men had an insatiable desire to gain knowledge throughout their entire lives! The average person learns the most while listening, reading or doing, how does Tangent Tom have any time left in his day for learning? Companies rely on innovative ideas to improve operations, expand into new areas and stay competitive. Sometimes these innovations are extremely complex such as a new and improved machine that provides a higher yield or an enhanced computer program that allows employees to look at information in new ways. But some of the most significant innovations are very simple. Putting a little adhesive on the back of a pad of notepaper created a huge new business opportunity for 3M. Keep an eye open for opportunities to be innovative and sooner or later you'll strike pay dirt.

"Think Outside the Box" but don't you dare "Do Anything out of the Box."

You will be told often by management to "Think outside of the box" which sounds like a great thing to do. The problem comes when you try to <u>do</u> something "Outside of the box." Say you come up with a really good idea; it's more than likely going to meet some serious resistance. In order get something really going with it; you may have to resort to the old seed planting technique. In this case, the more seeds that get planted the better the chance that something will grow. By telling several individuals about the potential of your concept, it may take root. Of course you would like to get some credit for your idea, but it may need some higher-up champions, who will be happy to take the credit for you, to get the ball rolling.

The Pigeon Hole

All of us tend to pigeonhole others just as they will tend to pigeon hole us. Which one of the little nicknames applies to you? Be as versatile as you can be and demonstrate your flexibility often. Master all you can at your place of employment as you have many years in which to accomplish this. If you become a little bored with your current position, look for one that will interest you and compliment your existing skills. Even if you love what you are doing, take some time out of each week to talk to people in other departments about their challenges and rewards. They will appreciate your interest and you will learn a great deal from them.

Be Politically Correct.

To a degree, this is an important topic and of course you can expect several hours of training on how to act properly. However, it can all be boiled down to the following old concepts. Be respectful of others and live your life by the golden rule. If you truly treat others, as you would want them to treat you, you can go home proud of yourself everyday. Don't worry about any other confusing depiction of what being politically correct might mean.

Are you in your "Right Mind or Left?"

Do you tend to be highly imaginative or do you rely on a keen sense of logic? Are you more task oriented or do you like to look at the big picture? Engineers tend to be very logical people where as marketing folks should be very imaginative. Obviously we need all types of people contributing in order to realize the best possible outcomes for a healthy organization. The point here is that people tend to be predominately either logical or creative. This is the essence of why some people just can't work with someone who is an opposite. The key again is to have a proper mix and to put the effort into understanding other points of view. If you are a highly logical person, try taking an art course. Likewise, if you tend to be very creative, try looking into some logical thinking exercises.

Learning to expand your horizons and increase the number of ways you can look at things will help you in many different ways. If nothing else, you will gain an appreciation for the contributions of others. Don't allow yourself to build any walls between yourself and any other employee. You don't need to become their best friend, but respect them for who they are. When you do this you will demonstrate a level of maturity far beyond your years.

8

Mindless Endeavors

For a young employee, there is a natural tendency to strive to be as efficient as possible. An important thing to remember is that there will be many circumstances that are out of your control and as you're asked to participate in many of the non value-added activities just keep reminding yourself that you are getting paid for these efforts. The following mindless endeavors will no doubt be among them:

Attending Meetings

Why is it that we never get invited to the meetings we would like to attend only to find out about them after they've concluded? Why is it that some people love to schedule meetings for every little topic imaginable? Do we accomplish anything at meetings? Take a mental note of the percentage of meetings that you attend that are well run with agendas sent out in advance, the right people in attendance and some progress actually made. It is quite likely that you will spend anywhere from 20 to 80% of your time in meetings. Since the old theory that two heads are better then one still holds true, the gathering of several individuals to work on a selected topic seems to make sense. So why is a good meeting such a rare thing?

The Weekly Report

The weekly report is written in order to provide a summary of what you are working on and a place to highlight any significant milestones achieved. They are typically consolidated and sent upstream where they will be consolidated further. Although this busywork may have some minor communication benefits, it has far more in terms of drawbacks. The first being that by the time anyone were to read one, it will be dated material. The second drawback is that nobody really reads the damn things. If something really important happened, the big cheese should already know about it. Whenever possible, I like to engage in a face-to-face conversation to discuss progress, hurdles or anything else for that matter. Without the benefits of seeing facial expressions and body language, communication is just not the same! You will be forced to write weeklies, so just do your best job. Using an outline style will minimize your time. That way, if anyone has a question, you will get your face-to-face opportunity. I once knew a gentleman who had a pension for writing weekly reports. He was so into this activity that his weeklies tended to be several pages long and they covered every topic imaginable. I think he missed his true calling in life, but I did learn a great deal by actually reading his!

Individual Development Plans

IDPs are designed by each employee to provide a guiding light for the employee's career development for the coming year. They are intended to provide a roadmap for career enhancement. They typically cover the educational progress that you are to achieve. Sounds like a great idea doesn't it? Here's the problem with IDPs. After completing the arduous task of putting your thoughts down on some funky template and having your boss ask you to revise it three times, you just won't care anymore what the damn thing says. As a result, you will commit to things that cannot possibly be accomplished in a dynamic environment. Although it's intended to be "individual", you will always be relying on others to help you accomplish your goals. These planning tools appear to be an offshoot of the old management by objectives era. Just don't let your supervisor forget that when the year is over, the most important thing is your actual results and not some piece of paper! More important than any development plan is a supervisor who is genuinely interested in helping you advance and these people are extremely rare!

Project Timesheets

This little gem is the pride and joy of the bean counters. The intent is for you to accurately record the time spent on your various projects as you go through your week. Well if you're an effective, multitasking contributor, this extra task could take up a third of your day. What is the value to your organization of this activity? Management will think it's a valuable tool for evaluating addition human resource needs. But in reality those decisions all boil down to the budget and quarterly results.

The Budgeting Process

If you have any interest in psychology, the "more me now" process of budget preparation should completely fascinate you. The first rule people learn when preparing a departmental budget is that it must be larger then last year. The only way to ensure that this will happen is to spend every penny, and then some, from last year's budget. It doesn't really matter what actually needs to happen or what expenditures are mandatory in order to achieve the departmental goals, this is the way budgets are always calculated. Take last years numbers and increase them by double of what you think they will cut in half during the budget review process. Now can you imagine a large company with hundreds of managers playing this game? Just for fun, try a little experiment at home and have all of your family members prepare a budget for next year.

9

Office Persuasion Techniques

For most of us, learning to be highly persuasive will take some time to perfect. Showing confidence in your own abilities should get you started in the right direction but to truly be convincing and motivating to other employees will require skills that can only be developed through much practice. Here are some common techniques that are used around the typical office.

Statistical Methods

Having solid data is often very important when trying to persuade others. It's hard to argue with numbers, especially when they are repeatable. Statistics are used extensively to strengthen many business studies. You will need to acknowledge the value of statistical tools as they have indeed helped to make major quality advancements over the years in many organizations. However, like any tool, proper use is very crucial. This fact is not well understood by very many people. Too often, stock is put into numbers that may fit a statistical model nicely even when they don't really get to the heart of the situation. Take, for example, your basic capability study. Determining a plus and minus 3 sigma capability for a given process certainly will provide useful information. But all too often the tolerances that are used in these formulas have been established with little or no investigation. If confronted with unfavorable results, By the Book Bob will experience total gridlock. For you, this situation could present a perfect opportunity to challenge the designer as to what was done to ensure proper tolerances were used. Ask them if they studied the capabilities of the process before assigning the tolerances, and you will most likely hear much stuttering. Statistics are useful and very boring. When making your presentations, use statistical tools but by all means downplay them as the only credible argument. It's very difficult to win someone over while they are asleep!

CC: Strategies

One of the most irritating situations you will experience, while working, is when certain people will not feel you are very important. Consequently they will blow you off when you ask for some small favor. This is totally unacceptable! When they say something like "sorry, I forgot" for the third time, you might need to consider using the dreaded CC strategy. I hate using this technique but have been forced to on several occasions. Some people use it everyday and that is overkill. But in certain situations, it can be very effective. As an example, I asked a colleague, in a different facility, to simply get a couple of signatures on a form so I could transfer a piece of equipment to him. I did this by email and he returned a "no problem" response. After a couple of weeks, I sent a reply, to his reply, which inquired as to his progress. After a few days, he replied with "it has already been signed and I will try to send it ASAP." The word "try" did not sit well in my stomach, but I gave him the benefit of the doubt. Of course I was right about the word "try" as nothing happened again. Having tired of this game, I sent the next email, which contained all of the previous ones, with the following wording. "I need you to send the signed form to me by Friday" and I copied his direct supervisor. I am sure he didn't enjoy this exercise, but I got what I needed and he had wasted enough of my time that I didn't care. If you find that you enjoy these games, read on as you probably have a bright future in management!

Annoying Surveys

Some of the service departments within your organization will periodically send out surveys inquiring what you think of their performance. This is usually done right after they completed a successful task or project for you. Treat these surveys like the act of making the coffee; just say no.

Expense Reports

You may be wondering why this topic falls under Office Persuasion. The main reason for this is that you'll need to persuade your supervisor to sign off on the damn things at the end of the month. Once you become a regular boondoggler, maybe you'll see what I mean. Anyway, one thing I found to be very helpful is to keep a simple daily log of expenses while on travel. If you don't, and you're gone for say a week or more, it can get very confusing trying to go back and account for all of the expenses you've incurred. Not only will you be confused, I guarantee that you will end up paying for something out of your own pocket and that is not in the true spirit of any boondoggle now is it? Your log will help immensely when filling out the necessary report when you get back to the office.

10

Recognition and Rewards

Just as the Golden Retriever lives for a simple pat on the back, employees need recognition for their hard work too. It can be very motivating when a supervisor is astute enough to give some well-timed and specific recognition for a job well done. Simply saying, "You're doing a great job" without a particular task being referenced, will not have the same affect. A little recognition can go a long way but oftentimes it can come under awkward circumstances.

Screw Ups, a "Good Thing"

Believe it or not, an occasional screw up or problem can offer a great opportunity for some positive recognition. This is not the formal kind of recognition that you may have been hoping for, but in the long run, this type can be more helpful to advancing your career. When a situation arises were there is imminent threat to progress on a top priority project or when manufacturing lines shut down, that gets attention. Coming up with a creative solution to these highly visible situations will pay huge dividends. If you manage your affairs so well that you never have any "situations," you may end up getting taken for granted!

The Review Process

Most supervisors and employees absolutely hate the annual review process. Constructing a summary of the past year's accomplishments can become an exhausting exercise when a supervisor has a number of reviews to do all at the same time. The best way I have found to approach this task is by having each employee complete his or her own annual review. It is amazing, but employees who try this will be more critical of their performance compared to the supervisor's evaluation. Criticism coming from another individual tends to upset us but we know where improvement is needed better then anyone, except possibly a spouse. When your supervisor does point out some of your weaknesses in a review, remember that it's part of their job and that they are probably right on some level. If you're caught a little off guard by something, calmly ask for clarification of their comments if you feel it's necessary. You can always add a comment from your perspective before you sign the document if it will make you feel better. Some of the clueless supervisors will wait until your review before they give you any feedback on your performance. If this is the case, you might be wise to ask them from time to time rather then wait. A smart jib will always work visibly much harder when they know the boss is working on reviews!

Compensation and Pay Increases

Compensation in today's world makes about as much sense as airline ticket pricing. It is supply and demand based to a degree but with some bizarre twists. Most companies use pay grades that are tied to similar positions relative to other industry in your same geographical region. Typically these are broken into pay bands based on a number or naming convention. These bands normally have a very large crossover at the low and high ends. It is important to be aware of this system because you will want to be positioned for the most potential gain. Here is how most companies utilize pay bands. After the review process is completed, you will receive one overall rating. This rating will become very important; as this is the number that will be used to calculate any pay increase you may receive. Managers are given guidelines that examine where you are in the pay band and what your rating is. The best scenario, for an increase, is to be low in your pay band with a high performance rating. The reason is that the pay bands are designed to have their mean match those other local companies. If people are not getting paid close to this target, then a company will be at risk of losing employees. However, once you reach this point, you are not likely to get future raises that amount to much more than a cost of living adjustment. The best way to significantly increase your income at that point will be to get moved into a higher pay band.

This rigid matrix approach to calculating compensation is created for the masses. Upper management folks will have a completely different set of rules. All you need to do is take a look at the business section of your local newspaper to read about multi-million dollar executive salaries. Now granted these individuals have a tremendous amount of responsibility, and their insights and long range vision can make a big difference. But are they really worth that much more than the average employee? You can be sure these folks are enjoying more boondoggles then you are. They have a real office with hard walls, a door, and windows with a view. They can have a phone conversation without fifty other people hearing what they say. What more do they need? Well evidently stock options and bonuses are what they crave! Gains on executive stock options can make up a huge amount of the total compensation for top CEOs. Of course your company will need competitive compensation in order to retain these talented individuals, but the potential gains they can realize are so significant that it might be impossible for them not to consider the impact of every business decision on their own personal gain. Many employees throughout your organization may be eligible for stock options, but it is highly unlikely that the quantity received will result in having their name listed in the newspaper next to the big dog. Lower level managers will tend to be under-compensated, just like you are, but they may have a little Management Incentive Pay thrown on top to make them feel like it's really worth all of the headaches.

Formal Recognition

Larger companies have several types of formal recognition. Sales contests, "years of service" and "employee of the month" are examples. Some recognition can be quite prestigious, lucrative and ongoing. Technical fellowships can fit into this description. So what's wrong with a little formal recognition you may ask? I would say almost everything. The "years of service" award isn't too bad but some employees make the assumption that they are a protected species after X number of years and that can be a big mistake. The huge problem with the other programs stems from the fact that for every one person that receives this type of recognition, many more do not. The end result is in de-motivating the masses while rewarding the few. The real sad part comes when you realize they spent a lot of money on an ugly plaque that you can only hang in the office because of the big company logo stuck on it. When you do, it only serves as a constant reminder to those other deserving individuals that they never seem to get any recognition.

Informal Recognition—Tickets for the game

This is the good stuff! When you receive tickets to the game, keep your mouth shut around the office. This is for two very good reasons. First, you can help control the jealousy thing by not advertising it. Second, if you talk too much about the game you may not receive them again so quickly because everyone will remember that you just got them recently. Even if you receive this perk because you're the only one that has the time free and can go, be very gracious in accepting them for the same reason as above.

Vacations

Ah vacations, the best time of the year. There is nothing like a long weekend or a week in the sun to recharge the old batteries. But why does the clock insist on running at such a fast pace during those precious days off? Have you noticed how few days off are granted anymore from the times when you where a kid? Are major historical events less important now or are we being snowed into fewer and fewer? Speaking of snow, you can't even hope for a snow day in this age of monster trucks with giant plows. Even a twenty-six inch overnight snowfall no longer presents a challenge to the daily grind. Americans are far behind the rest of the world in understanding the true essence of a good vacation. We are programmed to go see as much as possible in the shortest amount of time and we rarely stay in one place long enough to truly experience it. A seven-day adventure is considered a long vacation for the average American. For most other worldly traveler types, that is barely enough time to begin to relax! So who sits down to devise our short vacation schedules anyway? Have they no life of their own? Do they have no desire to allow us the ability to enrich our lives through the gift of travel? How is it that you must work for a company for so long before being granted another week of vacation? Why is there not a small vacation reward for each year of service? Why is it that only people who are too old to really enjoy travel seem to be the only ones with enough time and money to do it? The most puzzling question is why do some people use their vacation days to paint their house?

Options (Golden Handcuffs)

Receiving company stock options can be a real double-edged sword. Trust me, you should be on cloud nine the first and every time you receive an option to buy company stock through an option program. The drawback comes when these start forming a kind of golden handcuff. If staying with your organization is what you want, you could have a sweet deal going. However, if you start thinking about a career change to another organization, options can become a real complicating factor. That is exactly what they had in mind when these programs were designed.

Cash Bonus

No problems here, in the rare event you actually get one of these, just say thank you very much!!

11

Be Successful by Serving the Customer

One of the fastest ways for an employee to get noticed, in a good light, will be if they strive to provide excellent customer service to all of those, internal and external to the company, they interface with.

External Customers

It seems like the customer service I was accustomed to growing up is all but dead and gone these days. When you go out for dinner at a nice restaurant, even for a special occasion, often the waiter or waitress will only get a little friendly when it's time to calculate their tip. Recently, I was at a grocery store filling my cart to the brim. When I approached the cashier, she happened to be sitting on the belt where the food gets placed reading a weekly soap trash newspaper. The glare she gave me knowing she had to get off her ass was unbelievable! I think, if I wasn't in such shock, that I would have left the full cart right there and walked out. This is not the way to conduct yourself with customers under any circumstance and most people do find it appalling. Even if you're at odds with your supervisor or have some personal issue, do not go here. The best thing you can do to project a professional image is to provide exceptional customer service. In all cases give them a little more then they expect and you will blow your customers away. It is as easy as asking if there is anything else you can do for them after the business appears to be completed. If for any reason you cannot accommodate a request, apologize. At a fast food chain recently, a woman in line in front of me asked for biscuits and gravy for breakfast, the young person behind the counter barked back that we don't have biscuits, period. No apology, no explanation. It was said as if the woman should have known that they were out. In my mind, this simple act was grounds for termination! Sure there are customers out there that will seriously challenge your sanity, but remain polite and apologize again, on behalf of the company, if anything is out of your control.

Internal Customers

Even if you don't interface with outside customers directly, you can still give superior customer service to your internal customers. These are the people that really rely on your help to satisfy the end customer.

12

Getting your Big Break

Now that you have graduated from an idiot to a jib, providing excellent customer service no doubt, you will be noticed and be given a "real project." This is a big day! You probably had the knowledge for this assignment the day you walked in the door, but now that you have proven yourself and shown a good attitude, your chance to shine has finally come. Mine came in the form of a large business opportunity if we could break through some technical barriers in our production area. With the help of a few other team members, from different disciplines, we were able to break through those barriers and get a huge chunk of business from a very important customer. Even if your first project turns out to be a slam-dunk, recognize the significance of this situation and give it your best effort. If you happen to get an impossible project, keep in mind that something could be learned or gained that will help in future endeavors. Demonstrating a little tenacity, rather then throwing your hands up, is a good idea as the solution may become apparent at a later date. If not, you will be given another chance on attitude and professionalism alone. Although you will still be competing with other jibs, this is a good time to start developing the ability to work with others in your organization. A collaborative approach will be necessary to tackle most of the challenges thrown your way. If you have been kind to the people you've met and shown them respect, you will find they will be more than willing to help you in any way they can. If you have been pompous or degrading in any way, you will find that help may be very hard to come by. If your project includes implementing something completely new to your organization, try to involve all of the people that may be affected by the change later on. This action will help prevent unnecessary complaints down the road. Always remember to give credit to those who help you achieve your objectives.

13

Management Practice

This seems like a good place to start bashing management folks a little more don't you think? Not only is this fun but it's also easy to do.

Taking Time to Mingle with the Little People

Why is it that so few executives take the time to mingle with the worker bees? It seems to me that there is no better way to stay connected to what is really going on in your business. This is especially true if your company does some manufacturing on site. The most refreshing thing about people who actually have their hands on the products is that they will be happy to tell you what really needs to be done in order to improve things. Sure, they may take the opportunity to embellish on the situation, but that's OK. If you work in an organization where this never happens, consider the quality of information that gets to the top through all of those layers of filters. Top management folks obviously have very busy schedules, but those who make a little time to mingle on a regular basis will have a much clearer picture of what's really going on with their organization.

The Centralize/Decentralize Game

This game is the coveted ploy of many clueless CEOs. It's played all of the time in many different types of organizations. Basically, here's how it goes. You take a CEO who wants to make his or her presence known, yet they don't know a damn thing about how the organization really functions. The solution they seem to always come to is that they simply decide to centralize departments that are decentralized and they decentralize any that are centralized. Pure genius right? Well the funny thing is, that a few years later when the next clueless CEO is in place, it will all go back to the way it was! You may be asking yourself, what difference does this make as long as they stay out of my hair? Well if you consider the time and money that ends up going to fund these little maneuvers, it should be of no surprise to you when there is no cash left to give you that much deserved raise!

The Matrix Reporting Concept

After successful completion of the Centralize/Decentralize game, the clueless CEO will again become bored and want to find another way in which to "contribute" to the organization. If the company has been operating with traditional type departments for several years, it is prime for a Matrix Management experiment. Previously, if you were even slightly perturbed with your current supervisor, wait until you have two or three at the same time to deal with! Matrix Management must have been the brainchild of some frustrated ex-manager turned author and motivational speaker. The concept is rather simple and seems to make good sense from a 10,000 foot, uninvolved, view. But wait until you have the opportunity to experience it first hand. In the typical Matrix arrangement, you will continue to report to your department manager but will also report directly to one or more managers with "project" responsibilities. This may sound like a nice change of pace to you, especially if the old way was getting a little tiresome, but the problems will start to surface when it becomes evident that all of the project managers care only about the projects they are directly responsible for. These managers will frequently get into dogfights with each other in order to get the resources needed to complete their pet projects. A fascinating thing about this phase of the transition is that all of these wayward managers will lose any concept of "the big picture" that they may have once had. The other thing that will transpire is that they will no longer look upon their colleagues as allies or friends. The competition for resources will drive a wedge between the closest of them. A benefit of this situation for you will be that it will become rather easy to snow your original manager that you are currently working very hard for one of the other chiefs! The Matrix Management approach has become very popular at many companies today and the concept does offer some real advantages in management flexibility but it also adds to the confusion of who should be doing what. If you are aware of these facts, ahead of time, it will be quite easy for you to make the most of the situation by reducing your actual workload and at the same time making it appear that you have increased it simply by reporting to multiple leaders.

The Outsourcing Ploy

If your company falls into the trap, that most do sooner or later, it will end up giving far too much authority to the resident bean counters. When this happens, all kinds of bad decisions start getting made on a regular basis for all the wrong reasons. If you remember Finance Frank, all he really cares about are dollars going to the bottom line. Frank is not a risk taker and he certainly will not be in favor of any capital expenditures if upper management does not directly sanction and demand them. Frank believes that the company should be able to profit using antiquated equipment and facilities for an indefinite period of time. If the capital purse strings become too tight and the organization is still experiencing growth, a new way must be found in order to support manufacturing demands without actually buying any more equipment or increasing the "head count". The solution is to start outsourcing at an aggressive rate. These are good times for the purchasing departments as the gold card has once again been unleashed. Outsourcing can be made to sound very appealing to upper management types as it provides short-term answers to many of their pressing issues. What they don't stop to really consider is all of the long-term impacts these actions can have. For example, companies that utilize outsourcing can also inadvertently "outsource" some of their strategic plans and/or intellectual property. Although great care can be exercised in writing confidentiality agreements, people still love to talk and talk. It is truly amazing the amount of strategic information that can be learned from suppliers about the companies they do business with. This is not to say that a good outsourcing strategy is to be completely avoided, but knowing what and when to outsource can become extremely important. If these decisions are left entirely in the hands of finance and purchasing, your organization could be headed for big trouble!

If you think manufacturing is the only area vulnerable to outsourcing, you better think again. Many white-collar positions are also being outsourced thanks to advances in worldwide communication systems. Where and when will the pursuit for cheap labor ever end?

Companies claim to be community-minded yet they seldom factor the net loss of jobs in their local areas into the above actions. Try to come up with ways to improve your business while keeping employment in your community. People who can pull this off will be the true heroes of our future.

Loyalty, a two-way Street?

Most people are led to believe that loyalty is indeed a two way street. That being, if you are loyal to the organization that you are working for, the organization will be loyal to you. This is a myth! People, in management today, only care about their career advancement and you are only there to serve as a stepping-stone on their ascent up to a higher level of the bureaucracy. It is a very sad state of affairs when 10 to 30 year employees are let go because of corporate downsizing. Yet, this is an event that has become far too commonplace. Even more shocking is the way in which Wall Street tends to give short-term rewards to those organizations that publicly announce large reductions in their workforce. To me, this seems to be completely counter-intuitive. If a company performs so poorly that they need to lay off large blocks of employees, why on earth would you increase their stock valuation for poor results not only in the bottom line, but more importantly, in the human devastation that has just occurred? It is extremely irritating that some people realize financial gains during times of human misfortune.

Delegation

The art of proper delegation is one of the most important skills a good manager can master. Unfortunately, they tend to be on either ends of the spectrum when it comes to delegating. Some managers delegate virtually every task before them while others have trouble letting go of anything. An important thing for you to realize is that all managers delegate on sight. If you happen to be in the wrong place at the wrong time, you will be the lucky recipient of an extra task or two. If you stop in to visit your supervisor too frequently, they will start giving you a task with each visit merely out of convenience. The best way to avoid delegation is to stay out of sight!

Keeping Them under your Thumb

When it comes to managers, you will encounter far more dictators then you will coaches! This is a sad fact, as most employees would benefit much more from a good coach. The main problem lies in the fact that managerial types tend to be too easily threatened. When you think about it, this shouldn't surprise you. Many of the employees, underneath these uneasy managers, have their sights on their boss's job while at the same time, their supervisor's want to make sure that they are not replaced by some young new hot shot superstar. The whole system ends up having the effect of suppressing employees rather than encouraging them to succeed. If you're thinking about moving your career into the direction of middle management, think long and hard about the consequences of being continually "under the thumb" of the level above you while at the same time, getting flack from the level below. The thing is that the threat from below is real and sometimes results in unsettling reversals. The first time I witnessed a case of this my jaw hit the floor. The manager, at the time, happened to be a friend of mine and an extremely nice person. If he had a fault, it was that he had a little trouble making decisions quickly. The ironic thing was that he realized this shortcoming and so he hired a very decisive individual to assist him. His thinking was that the guy he ended up hiring would become the perfect teammate and business compliment, that he knew was needed. What ended up happening though, in just a short time, was that upper management was so impressed with the decision-making prowess of this new employee, that they promoted the guy and demoted the manager. This sent not only a little shock wave through the organization but also a huge message to the other managers. That being, unless you want this to happen to you, make sure you hire someone less competent and decisive than you are and keep them under your thumb. Can you see how this could create a kind of domino effect that would start to cause a downward spiral after only a few short years? It's not to say that there would be a total decline in competence, but the effect of thinking that this could happen to you next would have a tremendous effect on every waking thought of the rest of the management team. It would become, at the very least, difficult to perform their daily tasks with a clear head and a "coaching" style. No matter what your position in the company ends up being, you may feel like you're being kept "under the thumb" of someone you now know is just a little on edge for good reason.

Another way managers can keep employees "under their thumbs" is to kind of ignore their existence altogether. This type of manager becomes very frustrating later on when you become ready to climb the corporate ladder. These managers can be rather crafty and hard to identify because often they will appear as very good listeners. The reason they behave this way is because they totally rely on information, as well as any real work, to come from their subordinates. They view the people reporting to them as some kind of indentured servant rather then as a valuable corporate partner. These managers exist at all levels of the organization and the higher the level the more frustrating the results. If they reside, let's say, at the director level, they will rarely take the time to even meet the employees reporting to the managers below them. If you work for an organization for more than a year and you have not had a chance to meet the individual two steps up, it is not likely that you will receive any kind of true mentorship or help in advancing your career by your manager or your director. If you are the type of employee who is happy with your situation and have no desire to climb any further, you will be in luck. The reason for this is that your manager will be among the easiest to "snow." After building some rapport, they will believe anything you tell them, as they will have no other way to verify your story. They won't really be involved in the day-to-day activity so the only way for them to discount what you say would be if one of your colleagues where to squeal on you. This type of betrayal rarely happens as all of the people reporting to this putz are in the same boat and they will form a kind of code knowing that the support of their peers is the only type of comfort they are likely to enjoy. If you find yourself in this situation, about the best thing you can do is to enjoy as many boondoggles as you can muster until the inevitable happens and you get a new manager, which should not take too long. In the 22 years I have been working since graduating college, I have had 11 supervisors. Most of them I liked on a personal level but only a couple of them on a professional level! It is great working for many different people in a way because all of them will operate a little differently and you will learn about all of the things that shouldn't be done as well as a few things that you may appreciate.

Empire Building

You may be wondering how some of these neurotic mid level managers ever advance their careers. Well that's where a little ploy known as Empire Building comes into play. Rather than waiting for someone else to recognize their contributions and give them a promotion, they give it to themselves! The super thing about this trick is that they don't even have to be in their position very long before initiating the necessary activities. The key here is to eventually add a level below them to supervise the people in their group that seem a little too troublesome for them to deal with. This maneuver will accomplish two things. First, it will put a buffer between them and those special challenges. Second, it will create a level under them that will now be equal to the level where they were. By minimizing the number of direct reports they end up with, this manager can ensure that there will be plenty of time left to browse for brownies.

Monument Building

What business leader doesn't want to leave a lasting tribute to their success? Someday they may move on to greener pastures so how will their true genius be remembered? Even though the truth of the matter will have more to do with them being in the right place at the right time rather then the effect of their leadership efforts, they will have convinced themselves that they were directly responsible for the organization's growth. A larger then life golden statue fashioned in their image and located next to the main entrance may be a little over the top even for our little ego maniac. So what can they do? Well it seems the preferred solution is to either do a major face-lift to the buildings facade or build a new corporate building altogether. Naturally they will hire the finest of local architects to assist in this endeavor. By doing so, the project will no doubt go way over the initial budgetary figures but by this time our fearless leader will be so enamored by the whole thing that the budget will be readjusted accordingly. Here is where some of the real frustrations began. Now that the company has committed a serious amount of money to the project, it will become virtually impossible to get any funding for the things needed to run the damn thing. If the organization happens to be flush with cash, employees may take pride in a major construction project that physically demonstrates the success of the organization. But this pride can fade fast when they come to realize that the new facility is only intended to house the upper echelon.

You will find that learning how to manage your management is not only very important, but also very exhausting.

Keys to being a successful manager.

Although it can be very difficult to manage diverse groups of highly skilled and intelligent individuals, there are some sure fire things you can do as a supervisor to ensure your teams success.

Be Fair-

Fight for your people, environment, financial resources and your cause-
Set clear roles and responsibilities-

Demonstrate that you believe in what you're doing and not just taking the company for a ride-

Help your people develop themselves both formally and informally-

Stay in your position long enough to actually accomplish something meaningful-

Don't ever try to establish respect through intimidation-

Show that you're human and occasionally admit mistakes-

Act like a Golden Retriever with an attitude-

Hold your upper management as accountable as they hold you and your people-

Construct "healthy pyramids"-

Make well-informed decisions-

Be patient. If you're highly driven, disappointment will be ever present-

Value experience-

Solicit the opinions of quiet personnel-

Understand that everyone wants more pay and more say. Make it happen-

Remember that it's lonely at the top-

Know that too much challenge and pressure will make people act in strange and unproductive ways-

Foster good competition-

Recognize contributions with specific and relevant feedback-

Don't alienate employees by overlooking anyone-

Do not look for quick fixes or panaceas, they do not exist-

Try not to insult intelligence-

Have fun with people-

14

Choosing your Path

As discussed last chapter, it can be tough duty to enter the realm of middle management, but some will find a perfect home there. If you were born to coach, mentor and lead with no fear of being run over by subordinates, then management is for you! If you're looking at a supervisory career merely because it seems like the best place to be to advance your income, you may want to reconsider what is really going to become important in your life. In my career, I went from being an engineer to a supervisor. After nearly 10 years of management duties, I got the chance to go back to engineering for a great company and the decision was easy. Sure I missed some of the perks that went along with being a designated leader, but soon realized that I didn't miss all of the headaches and countless hours of back-to-back meetings that came with them. Besides, it seemed more gratifying and challenging to me to provide leadership through good logical thinking and hard work. It's kind of funny but I had come to dislike the automatic respect that came with the title alone. Being treated like some kind of celebrity merely because people want to stay on your good side is nice at first but fades relatively quickly when you begin to realize just how hollow this feeling really is. Fortunately more and more companies are starting to embrace the importance of dual ladder systems. Whether you choose a technical path or a supervisory one, you will want to advance your career so having a good structure to facilitate the journey is very important. As you are researching the companies you might want to work for, make sure you take a close look at the ladder systems within various organizations. This will give you a window into how important your advancement will be to a given employer. If you have chosen a path that is neither technical nor supervisory, there doesn't seem to have been as much effort placed on creating formal structures for advancement. For example, take a look at how many different levels of sales representative do you find? Yet if sales is your chosen field, I am quite sure you will advance your skills and value to your organization as the years go by. But how will this be reflected in your title, compensation and responsibilities? I encourage everyone reading this book to challenge their human resource departments with doing a better job of recognizing the basic human needs associated with proper experience and contribution recognition. So many organizations have bought into the old Manage by Objectives mantras but very few seem to go beyond this and reward based on true accomplishment. Think about what you really enjoy doing and let that be your guide for choosing a career path rather then someone else's image of what makes a successful individual. This is easier said then done as the values of important people in our lives always enter into these decisions. If you're lucky, you may get the opportunity to try working for different departments before settling in on a home. Many companies offer rotation programs to recent graduates. These programs provide a great method of getting introduced to an organization by allowing you to work with several different people who will be responsible for a tremendously large variety of projects. One of the best features of the program is that if you get a real jerk for a boss, you know you will get to rotate out and move to a new one soon.

15

Climbing the Ladder

In order to start climbing that old company ladder, you may need to somehow convince your higher up that you're ready for that next step. There are a few things that you can do to hedge your bet in this situation, but ultimately, it is someone else's call. If your supervisor is in any way threatened by your getting a promotion, it will not happen unless they feel a little pressure to make the change from above. This is a situation that does not bode well for any of the parties involved, as it will invariably leave a bad taste in someone's mouth. The best way to approach the subject is in a calm and factual manner. First off, slowly start dropping hints that you're a little anxious to achieve the next level. Next, start communicating with your Humane Resources Department in order to get a written description of what it means to be at that next position. If there are quantifiable requirements, such as education or X number of years experience, make sure you have them or at least good rational of how you have satisfied them. When you think about it, these milestones are, and should be, nonnegotiable. They established the ground rules for fair play in the past and if they were breached now, it would cause much consternation on behalf of those whom have already run the same gauntlet. Climbing the ladder is a very important thing to all employees as it in some ways satisfies a basic need to feel that you are accepted, appreciated and valued for your years of contributions. It is very unfortunate that the typical Humane Resources Department has lost sight of this very powerful and potentially motivating fact. In most companies, there are far too few classifications of each job type. In some cases, there are no graduated steps at all. Think of how this differs from your years in the academic arena. How about your college days and how the difference between freshmen, sophomores, juniors and seniors was so obvious. You know that with each year of education or work experience, much is learned that will benefit a person's ability to apply wisdom to those difficult decisions that are made every day. How can this not be reflected in employees' annual reviews? Another pet peeve is the fact that most Humane

Resources "Professionals" completely miss the boat when it comes to recognizing excellent performers who may not have the token sheep skin necessary to properly acknowledge such a star. This is very common among technical contributors that may be lacking an engineering degree. For that matter, why do other employees enjoy so much recognition simply because they attended a college of distinction? The fact that their families' financial status allowed such a luxury does not mean they will provide the type of contributions that one would expect. The most innovative engineer I have ever met and had the pleasure of working with, did not even go to college. Many companies today will not allow the use of an engineering title for employees that do not posses a college degree. While I agree that it is important to recognize those who have completed difficult course work, it seems unconscionable to me that no company has come up with a good title for people who fit the above description! The default, in this case, seems to always be the title of technician or aide. These titles, although they describe very important roles, typically do not carry the financial rewards or perks that many of these employees deserve. The net result is that some of the best employees can become de-motivated over a stupid title. I have often wondered how effective it might be to abolish all titles within an organization and replace them with a system that would provide a feeling of equal importance to all contributing employees.

16

On a Serious Note

Although many of the people you work with may tend to drive you crazy and the red tape of the office will seem endless some days, it is good to reflect, from time to time, on how lucky you are to be gainfully employed. Although there is much improvement to be made in the corporate world, there are many people around the globe who would love to have the opportunity to complain about this and that around the water cooler. It is also very important to have a little fun and find some enjoyment every day we are at work. It is very easy to get stressed out when projects are numerous and timelines are too short so take some time to get away during your break. It is sad to see so many employees eating lunch at their desks as they continue to slave away. Some of the nicest people work hard their entire career and sadly pass away shortly after retirement. Being cheated out of the golden years seems like such an unfair conclusion for these folks.

17

Glass Ceilings

If you find yourself working in a privately held organization, you need to be aware of the fact that you more than likely will encounter a glass ceiling at some time in your career. Although Glass Ceilings are not nearly as obvious as they once were, they still exist at many different levels. If you are a highly driven individual, hitting one of these will be most aggravating. Even more aggravating will be witnessing a friend or family member of the owner pass smoothly through this barrier. Glass Ceilings have been placed over employees' heads in both public and private companies for reasons of gender, race, religion, etc. If you look at the longevity of privately held family businesses you will discover that they rarely last for more then 3 generations. If you think about how much passion the original owners must have had to build a strong organization from scratch, it is truly admirable. It is unfortunate that this passion rarely gets passed down through the generations.

18

Getting Back to the Basics

Staying focused on the basics of a business is no longer as straight forward as it once was. This is especially true in huge companies that serve thousands of people throughout the world. With layers and layers of management and hundreds of products to offer, the complexities become mind-boggling. Yet staying focused on the basics is always of top importance to survival. Companies rely heavily on Mission Statements to help their employees stay aligned but these can seem so vague to the average Joe. Often times, large groups of managers will attend offsite meetings at fancy retreats for several days trying to develop words of wisdom only to bring back some ridiculous statement. So what can you do as an individual contributor to ensure your company succeeds? Provide excellent customer service. Have a passion for what you do and think about how you contribute to the bottom line. Be open to new ideas. Challenge traditional thinking. Have some fun.

19

Watching others Wind Down &
Attending Retirement Parties

It is such a blast to work with people who are getting close to retirement. They smile all of the time. They aren't too afraid to make a few well-timed derogatory comments. They seem to move through the office with less effort then they did before. But most noticeable is how forgiving they can be of situations that tend to drive everybody else nuts. You can really see that there has been some kind of invisible weight lifted from their shoulders.

Celebrating a retirement can conger up many mixed emotions. On one hand, they now have the freedom of how they spend their days. They have plenty of time to visit with friends and relatives. Getting a tee time at their favorite golf course sure is a lot easier mid-week than it is on the weekends. On the other hand, they no longer are working at a job that they had so much passion for. The people they enjoy working with will be by far the hardest to leave behind.

It seems so anti-climactic when you attend a typical retirement party in a large company.
Sure there may be a cake, fruit and some coffee. Most everybody who even remotely knew the retiree will stop by and make some small talk and say good luck. But after so many years of dedication, it just seems like there should be something more. How the hell will this place ever run without them? Well, nonetheless, it's time for them to start a new chapter in their life.

20

Keeping Some Balance

People's lives have become so busy today that it is almost impossible to find the time to do all of the things we would like to do. Commutes to and from work have gotten longer; the workweek certainly hasn't gotten any shorter. More and more, both husband and wife work full time in order to pay the mortgage and feed the kids. Children are more involved in extracurricular sporting activities. In many ways it is great to be so active but do we have any time left in our lives to stop and smell the roses? Everything seems to move in fast motion, they way we drive, the way we work, even the speed with which we talk seems to be faster these days. Our only real down time comes at that time of the day when we are too exhausted to stand up anymore until the time we pass out for a few hours of sleep. Snapping on the television has become a conditioned response. Fighting over the remote almost a national pastime. Many of us are stressed out, at least slightly over weight and to be sure, somewhat out of shape. When was the last time you actually experienced a day of boredom? We have cell phones so that we can keep talking, laptop computers so we can keep working and pagers so that even our lunch breaks can be interrupted. We absolutely crave fast food. Children definitely seem to be growing up faster these days. When we finally do get a chance to relax what do we do? We go the movies to watch our favorite stars, drive fast, east fast, love fast, engage in fast action and then die fast. More then likely, the word "Fast" will even appear in the title of the movie. We have instant coffee, microwave ovens, high-speed Internet lines, bullet trains and super sonic jets. We want our careers to be on the fast track. Why are we in such a hurry? Is there anything we can do to slow the pace down just a bit? Some of life's simple pleasures can be just the ticket if you place a little priority on carving out a few hours on a regular basis. When is the last time you sat around a campfire to just watch the flames dance around? Or closed your eyes and listened to the wind blow? Take a day off and do something completely by yourself. Paddle a canoe on a quiet lake. Go for a walk. Gaze at water flowing in a nearby creek. Try slow cooking a meal. Go to the museum. It might be a good idea to try and balance a few slower paced things into your fast paced life.

21

Life as a "Senior" Jib, Is Danger Lurking?

By now you have mastered the art of survival in the corporate world. You have practiced avoiding delegation. You have browsed for many brownies and hopefully have enjoyed some wonderful boondoggles. You have come to appreciate the drab office environment. You have separated yourself from the other jibs and established yourself as a valuable contributor. Congratulations, for you now can be considered a senior jib. How many crazy things have you seen? How many times have you been reorganized? How many supervisors have come and gone during your tenure? Have you learned any new office persuasion techniques? Has your company grown and will your stock price reflect the fruits of so much effort? How many times did you have to use the phrase "I never did mind about the little things" to survive? Well take a moment to sit back, relax and give yourself a little pat on the back you senior jib you. Yes your burlap kennel is still the same size and there is no artwork anywhere to be seen, but it should feel like home by now. You probably will have become immune to a lot of those little things that you noticed earlier on in your career anyway. So where do you go from here? You have reached the salary mean in your pay band so there won't be any more significant raises. You have achieved the peak level of competence in your field and you just don't have the stomach to supervise a large group of idiots and jibs. Well good luck coasting for a while! Early warning signs of trouble brewing on the horizon become apparent when you suddenly hear your supervisor start to use phrases like, we need to think about how we can reinvent ourselves or I think we should consider new ways how our department can become more flexible and responsive. Yes, you know that change is inevitable but why does it have to come now that you're a relaxed senior jib?

What will it be this time, more outsourcing, another reorganization, added responsibilities or downsizing? Downsizing and head count reductions are among the most dreaded words for any employee. It all comes down to making the numbers. Getting let go from a company is a tragic thing. Sometimes organizations will drop the ax right before a holiday season in the hopes that people will have a support group during this time. Don't they realize that holidays are stressful enough on their own? Gone are the days of early retirement packages and right sizing through natural attrition. Are small layoffs better than one big one? Having one small layoff after another really makes people wonder when is this ever going to end and who is next? Sometimes companies will ask their employees to give concessions during the tough times. This concept might be somewhat more palatable if it applied to the executives as well. Chances are good that you will experience tough economic times in your career so always keep in mind that this is a possibility. One of the low points in my career came when I was asked to revoke the raises I had just communicated to 12 employees. Maybe it wouldn't have been quite so hard to do if the owner hadn't just bought a new jet. Getting let go at any point in a career is a tough pill to swallow, but for a senior jib it can be particularly difficult.

It is very interesting observing people in the office during layoff situations. For the lucky ones, not directly affected, go through a process beginning with shock, then relief, then guilt and finally some employees start to even rationalize why so and so were the ones to go. I think that it's just a way of reassuring themselves that they couldn't be next. There was an article in the local newspaper recently about a guy who felt so guilty about not being one of the thousands of people let go from his organization that he just quit on his own. Evidently, he couldn't feel good about going to work anymore after what he had witnessed. Another employee from the same company had elected to take a demotion rather than get let go but was now living with the guilt of knowing that someone else, with less seniority, was a casualty of his decision.

Some people who get let go eventually end up much better off then they were for one reason or another. Some find less stressful jobs. Some look at new careers that they may not have thought to look into otherwise. Some have a damn hard time finding something new. One of the harsher realities, during this difficult time, lies in the fact that your unemployment check may not be enough to even cover your monthly health care costs while looking for a new opportunity.

Hang in there for soon you will be an employed jib once again and at that point you might even be thinking it would have been nice to have a little more time off!

22

Reminiscing about the Good Old Days!

When you get the chance, ask as many senior jibs as you can about what they considered the good old days. If you can catch them at the right time and in the right frame of mind, you will be amazed at the stories they will tell. Companies can change a great deal over a period of 10 to 20 years and so do people. You might be astonished to find out who the wild ones were in your office and just what kind of crazy stunts they may have pulled.

Corporate life was a little different back in the early nineteen eighties when I was fortunate enough to land my first "real" job. The position was listed in the local newspaper and it sounded like a perfect fit for what I was looking for. The interviewing process went quite favorably and I was ecstatic when an offer was made. After accepting the position, there was a great sense of relief having spent several months of applying at many different locations. The company was a midsized privately held organization that had an excellent reputation in the industry. It was experiencing growth and had an excellent benefits package. What wasn't apparent at this time was how closely knit the people were.

The company and its owner took great pride in the fact it had a corporate jet among its assets. It was used for travel between the different manufacturing sites as well as visiting customers, vendors, trade shows, etc. After working for the company for only a short time, I had a chance to fill an open seat and visit two of the facilities, each in a different neighboring state, all in one day and be home in time for dinner. On the final flight back, I was delighted to find that there was cold beer, and other drinks, available after a hard days work. This was living, sitting back to enjoy a cold beer while paging through an educational men's magazine on a corporate jet! I remember thinking, just a few short weeks ago, I was a broke kid looking for a job, any job.

Back then; mixing booze and business was a very common practice. A couple of bumps at lunch was the norm if out with managers or entertaining customers. You could find a group of co-workers going out for happy hour after work at one of the many local establishments almost every night of the week if you asked around. Good thing I was single and had learned how to consume my share during school. Could it get any better? Well with all of the parties and happy hours, there certainly was enough social interaction to keep the gossipers busy!

Chain-smoking was practiced by nearly every member of the meetings I would attend. Ten of us would pile into a tiny conference room and nine would immediately light up. Smoking was one habit I had managed to avoid but the second hand smoke we were exposed to in those little rooms, with no ventilation, was incredible. It was astounding to look up and see just how yellow the ceiling tiles had gotten over the years.

The smoke was bad but the coffee may have even been worse. Coffee was a necessity after the late nights of entertainment so pouring down ten to fifteen cups a day was fairly normal. In addition to the caffeine boost we got, it turned out that it was a pretty good floor cleaner as was demonstrated to me, on a nasty stain on the floor of the production office, one day. Apparently the regular cleaner hadn't touched this stain so one of the old timers just poured a little coffee on it and gave it a quick wipe with a shop towel and it was gone!

Golf was a very important vehicle for communication. Playing on the company league was the best way for a young employee to get a chance to mingle with the brass and find out what was going on with all of the various departments. If you didn't play golf, you just couldn't be in the know. Of course, there was plenty of beer to cool us off on those hot summer days. During the winter, the bowling league was the place to be. I know, bowling does not come to mind when you think about serious business getting done but for us it did. The main reason bowling had become so popular was that the president of the organization found it very important to be there and mingle nearly every week. He had a booming voice and would just love to heckle his opponents of the day. It didn't matter whether you were a good bowler as long as you'd show up and have a few cold ones.

The vocabulary used in industry at that time was a little different then what you might be accustomed to today. Frequent swearing was not only accepted but was fairly effective in getting people motivated.

Enough of the fond memories as you're probably waiting for some of those good senior jib stories.

We had the privilege of having a tremendous guy work for the company for several years and I'll call him John. I didn't get to work directly with John during his more active years but over time his adoring buddies revealed a few of his finer antics. Prior to owning the company jet, there was a prop plane that was used for travel and it was also available for those who wished to learn to fly. In fact, many of the senior jibs were encouraged to take this activity up. Anyway, shortly before I was hired, this practice was no longer encouraged after John had a bit of a tough landing. This unfortunate piece of news was about the first thing anyone had told me about John and my first impression was that this guy had just screwed up a really awesome perk. But the best story ever told about John had to do with an automobile. As the story goes, John had been at an informal outdoor get together where the booze had been flowing at the normal high rate. After several hours of indulgence, the weather started to turn and, when the rain began to pour down, John thought it might be a good idea to head on home. As he got in the car and put on the seat belt the skies really opened up and in no time the ground had started to get soft. So John turned on his windshield wipers and started on his way. He hadn't gone very far when he happened to get stuck in the mud with his back wheels just spinning. John wasn't aware of the fact that he was stuck so he just kept on driving keeping a careful eye on the dark road ahead of him. One of John's buddies watched in amazement as the wheels continued to spin and spin. Finally the buddy figured he better jump in the car and let John know he had a little predicament. When he did, John looked over at him and started a conversation. After just a few words, John suddenly got scared to death and said, "How in the hell did you get in here?"

One of our other esteemed employees, again with "the thirst" of course, came up with a real clever line one evening. He had been traveling for business and bad weather had prevented his flight from getting home. After landing in a different city, his party made hotel arrangements for the evening and decided to meet in the bar to kill some time. Well as you can guess, they had plenty of time to kill!

After several libations had been consumed, one of the other party members asked him if he had remembered to call his wife to inform her of the delay. As he was normally quite diligent about communicating with his better half, he felt rather embarrassed that this time it had slipped his mind. As it was well into the evening at this point, he concluded that she might be worried and that he better make some kind of contact. Somehow, in his condition, he realized that he had probably had a bit too much and didn't want to convey it over the phone. In his infinite wisdom, the solution came to him as he simply called home and when his wife answered he said, "Honey don't pay the ransom, I escaped!" Then he hung up.

If you try to relive these good old days, be smart and take a taxi home afterwards.

We tend to remember the best times from the "good old days" and thankfully forget some of the not so good. One thing is for certain though and that is that the good old days don't last forever. When the time came for me to leave this organization, it was a lot harder to say goodbye than I ever thought it would be.

23

Firing the Company

Now that you been around awhile, you may start to think does this company have a bright future? Are there enough advancement opportunities to keep me motivated as an employee? Did it start to feel like you've hit one of those glass ceilings and there just doesn't seem to be anything you can do to get through it? Do you find yourself torn between feeling lucky to be employed yet thinking there has got to be something better out there? Are you just having another one of those days or is the grass really greener somewhere else? Well sometimes it is and sometimes it isn't but one thing is for sure, if you've gotten to the point you just need a change, try to do it in a smart way. Especially if the handwriting is on the wall and your company has taken a turn for the worse. Do you want to sit around and participate in some kind of slow death that will have no added benefits for your loyalty? The key is to keep yourself in the driver's seat as much as possible. If the economy is in good shape and there are plenty of jobs available, this will definitely be in your favor. If things are a little tough out there, it is even more important to be prepared if something attractive comes along. One of the things you have been smart about is that you have been contributing to your 401k plan and you are fully vested right? These plans, especially if there is a company match, offer a great way to start accumulating funds for your golden years. If you are fully vested in your funds you will be able to roll them over when you find a new job. If you leave before you are fully vested you will stand to loose a good percentage of the money that is in your account. Also keep this in mind when your investigating prospective new companies by looking at the ones you will be likely to want to stay with for at least as long as the vesting period. Although by leaving your organization you technically have "fired the company" you'll want to be smart by not burning any bridges if at all possible. Of course you may be tempted to say good riddance, but you never know what the future might hold. Besides, you should be feeling all the satisfaction you need just by knowing you've found something better.

People change jobs much more frequently today then they used to several years ago. The reasons are many and it is an interesting topic. By working for more than one company, certainly you can learn more things and should become more valuable as an employee. Often people learn an expertise at one organization that is needed by another organization and they are given lucrative offers to jump the fence. If the expertise they have learned is in high demand, a Headhunter who has been contracted to find such individuals may contact them. Headhunters tend to be very bold individuals. They know that there is good money to be made on the brokering of talented individuals. They also know that time is of the essence in their profession. Headhunters have many techniques for finding the individuals they are looking for and they can be quite resourceful in their endeavor. Do not be surprised if such individuals contact you at home or at the office. When they do get a hold of you they will have a long list of questions regarding your education, work experience and will want to know all about your total compensation package. Even if you're not currently considering a change, it might be a good idea to keep a list of the names and telephone numbers of these irritating people just in case you may need their services in the future.

24

How does it all Work?

With all the crazy things that go on in corporations, how at the end of the day do they actually work? How can such a diverse work force come together and turn a profit? How can there be any kind of alignment when upper management is so removed and there is infighting among the lower ranks? What will the future bring after we outsource this operation, lean out that operation and reinvent the rest? Is bigger really that much better? How can we stay profitable with tier after tier of escalating salaries the further the pyramid raises? If we continue to move labor-intensive jobs to lower cost centers of the world when will it end and what will be left? One could spend an entire lifetime trying to find the answers to these questions. How would your company answer the following ones?

Who are our customers?
What do they want?
Are we giving it to them?
Are we giving them even more than what they ask for?
Do we offer competitive pricing?
Do we provide exceptional customer service?
Do we have superior products?
Are they coming back for more?
Do we listen to our employees?
Have we created an environment conducive to productivity?

25

About Teamwork

Take a few minutes to consider the following statements.

Developing effective teams is a monumental challenge.
Good teamwork is essential in order for organizations to maximize their potential.
Don't assign a team to what an individual can do.
Ensure the team has the proper make-up.
There is no "I" in team.
There is no "we" in team either.
Make sure all of the team members are actively participating.
It's a good idea to engage in team-building activities.
Teams tend to be inefficient.
There is a fair amount of synergy that can come from a team environment.
We have the best damn team in the business.
Our team just doesn't seem to mesh very well.
I'm on too many teams right now to get anything done.
Oh goody another team meeting!
Do you have a winning team?

The complexities around assembling a good team, keeping them motivated and disbanding them when the time comes are many. Yet everyone knows that good teamwork is essential for growth. In sporting events, teams typically have a scoreboard that reflects how well they are performing against their competition. But in the office, it is often times very difficult to discern how a particular team is performing.

I visited a company on the west coast one time that had a fairly interesting approach to using teams. What they were doing was setting up more then one team to achieve the same objective. The teams were to compete on the best design for the same end product. The winning team was to be determined by the cost to manufacture the product, how well it performed during testing and the overall aesthetic appearance. The relationships that resulted within these teams and between these teams were kind of interesting. Of course each team had designated spies to keep an eye on what the other team was doing which seemed to add to the fun they were having. What was most impressive about this arrangement was that all of the participants knew that no matter which design ended up being chosen, that they all would be winners in the long run. I was quite amused to speak with members of each team, as they would say things like the other team has a very elegant approach, but of course ours will win. Having a little friendly competition going certainly got these employees more excited about coming to work.

Team dynamics can be extremely interesting to study. Many times a strong team leader will emerge and take over a team. Sometimes this is exactly what is needed and other times it can kill the potential of the team. More than likely you will be involved with effective teams and some that are not so effective. One thing is for sure and that is every group of people assembled for a team will be unique so it is a good idea to be creative and try a few different types of meeting formats. Some team participants will sit perfectly quiet until they are directly asked for their opinion. Often, when this happens, what they respond with is so significant you will be baffled as to why they hadn't spoken up earlier! Try to observe the things that tend to get people to participate in meeting settings and you will become a better team member and leader when the time comes. Just getting team members to your meetings, starting them on time and staying focused can be extremely challenging so try to set the ground rules early about your expectations. Remember their time is as valuable as yours is so keep your meetings as short and to the point as possible.

26

Blowin' off a little Steam

Show me an employee and I'll show you a frustrated employee.

We all build up frustration at work. We are under great pressure to get too many things done in a timely manner and there are so many roadblocks that make even the seemingly simple tasks into monumental ones. It's only natural that this constant stress can take a toll on us after a while. The key is finding a good outlet for your frustrations before they become overwhelming. If you work with someone who isn't expressing some periodic intense frustration, it is quite likely that they have silently passed away in their burlap kennel without anyone taking notice. Why is it that the more of a hurry you're in the more things tend to go wrong? The copier is out of toner. The coffee pot is empty again. Bob wants just one more modification before he'll sign that report. The bulb in the overhead burned out. Your computer crashed again and you forgot to save your work. The timeline on your toughest project just got pulled in. Someone else got the position you really wanted. We have just one more little design change and then it will be frozen I promise. One of the most ironic things is that even being bored can also cause tremendous stress for an employee. Employees at all levels feel frustration to be sure. However the definition of "appropriate" outlet may differ depending on rank. Here are some of the frustration outlets I have observed over the years.

Business Owner.

Taking the jet to go skiing in Aspen for the weekend, again.
Yelling at unsuspecting employees.

Vice Presidents.

Putting their fist through the wall in their office.

Breaking the telephone receiver in half from slamming it down too hard.
Yelling at unsuspecting employees.

Managers.

Throwing their golf clubs in the pond.
Chain-smoking cigarettes.
Bending a golf club around a tree.
Drinking heavily.
Yelling at unsuspecting employees.

General Employees.

Breaking a pencil.

It seems as though there aren't as many outlets for those who don't have subordinates to yell at! Maybe they could try yelling at unsuspecting family members when they get home.

27

Getting Called to the Office

Getting called to the principal's office is a traumatic experience for any young student. Getting called to the boss's office can be highly reminiscent of those earlier days. Employees absolutely hate to be singled out and brought into the office for a little chat. If the door is closed after entering, you can be assured that the little lecture you're about to receive will turn your stomach. Sure there is an outside chance that you could get some good news in this same scenario but let's play the odds here. Despite your best efforts, there are just too many opportunities for misunderstanding or miscommunication to not eventually end up in a situation where you're given at least a little advise on how to conduct yourself in the future. When you find yourself in this situation it is best to not get defensive, as this will only make the situation worse. A response of "I'll do better in the future" should serve you fairly well in most cases. The first time I was called into one of these sessions provided me quite a little shock. Apparently the fact that I was leaving the office at 5 pm on Fridays during the summer was causing some concern on my boss's behalf that I was not very dedicated to the mission. I found it very interesting that, in a company where the owner's favorite saying was to "work smarter and not harder," this was an issue. When you live in a part of the country that has only 3 months out of the year with warm weather, weekends are a very precious commodity. Nevertheless, I promised to do better in the future knowing that winter was coming and I would be happy to show my dedication by working to 5:01. Try to remain calm, cool and collected as in some cases the reason you have been called to the office will be in complete error and the situation will then become quite embarrassing for your supervisor. A friend of mine was called into his boss's office to actually be terminated for allegedly using his corporate purchasing card to fund personal expenses. As it turned out, the guy hadn't even looked into the facts enough to realize that all of the charges he had made were for legitimate business expenditures!

In other cases, employees I know have gotten called into the interrogation chamber for upsetting other employees. One thing is for sure, in this day and age of trying to be sensitive to other people's feelings, personal interactions have become a great deal more complex. Even for those who try their best, it can be rather easy to unknowingly offend others. Certainly strict harassment laws have helped to increase employee awareness and prevent abusive situations but they have also provided extra stress on employees just wanting to enjoy some lighthearted fun at no ones expense. Be professional and stay away from any hint of saying or doing anything that could be remotely considered offensive to anyone. Appling a fresh strip of duct tape to your mouth every morning has proven somewhat effective in reducing comments in poor taste.

28

Breaking into the Inner Circle

We mentioned earlier how few people really make the major decisions in the typical company. What happens if you get tired of sitting on the sidelines and want to join in the real game? It can be very difficult to break into the inner circle of decision makers but it can certainly be done. Hard work, longevity, tenacity and most of all luck will be required. It can take many years of fostering relationships with other decision makers before you will be recognized for your insight and dedication. Up until now, you have had to rely on some well-timed seed planting in order to influence any significant decisions. But the time may come when you will want to become one of the bigger fish. Be sure of what you ask for as you might end up getting it (and more). Transitioning to a position of higher responsibility can result in some truly unexpected side affects. Some companies may have you relocated to another geographical area to gain more experience. Some employees find that making one of these transitions can result in an eventual downturn in their career. A few will survive the gauntlet to enjoy the loftier levels of the pyramid. Some of the more sarcastic jibs refer to this process as rising to your appropriate level of incompetence.

29

Ignorance is Bliss

Ignorance is Bliss—too bad it doesn't last!

I find politics can become very tiresome after a short while and office politics are no exception. A tremendous amount of energy can be spent just fighting the political battle du Jour. It's no wonder that most people get to the point where they just want to come to work, do their thing and then go home with as little disruption as possible. Why are there so many political roadblocks to the theoretical smooth sailing most of us crave? Have the smarter jibs come to realize that ignorance is bliss? How in the world can you hope to avoid all of the little power struggles that will be ever-present in dealing with numerous other employees? Is flying just below the political radar the best way to go? Many people have gone from being good friends to bitter enemies over differences of opinion on how things should be handled at the office. Do not be surprised when your organization transitions from a period of political stability to a time of intense instability. One of the biggest triggers for volatility can come when a high-ranking member leaves the organization. Filling the void that was created by the loss of a strong leader can result in bitter competition by those who feel they should be entitled to a shot at it next. If there are several individuals who feel that they should be the next successor, the final decision will be very difficult on those not chosen. Often times, the tension will be so intense that the company will have no other choice then to bring in an individual from the outside. In these situations, the outsider will have a very difficult time rallying the troops to function as one big happy family again! Maintaining a neutral position can be difficult to do, especially if you work closely with any of the affected individuals, but taking sides with anyone in particular may cause you some big problems down the road. If you can, try to sit back and enjoy the show, as it can be quite fascinating to witness business professionals acting just like children fighting over a coveted toy.

Enjoying life as a small cog in a giant wheel can be a much less stressful way to go but if you enjoy the thought of becoming a political warrior, you will have ample opportunity to fight countless battles in the days ahead.

30

Plan on Working Forever?

One of the most disturbing topics in the news these days is the trend towards working longer before retirement. With health care costs soaring and the fate of social security uncertain, there may be a need for employees to continue their careers long beyond the age that they had originally planned for. Now if you're reaching those golden years and you still enjoy what you're doing, good for you. But the thought of "working for the man" while a person is in their seventies and beyond, seems like cruel and unusual punishment. Who wants to go from a senior jib to a grandpa or grandma jib? Will funeral arrangements be added to the list of employee assistance programs? What's next? Will child labor laws be modified so that our children will be expected to enter the work force too?

We are living in such a fast moving dynamic world now that it's hard to imagine how many jobs will even be available in the future and what they will be like. Companies have learned how to be so much more productive than they ever were yet as employees we need to work harder then ever to continue to compete. Consider the shift in the percentage of people in this country that used to be involved with farming. As equipment improved and the corporate farms proliferated, many people were employed in the manufacturing arenas. Now with more automation and outsourcing, the service industries appear to be were the action is. What long term effects will the Internet have on the way we do business? What will be the result of global competition mixed with a huge dose of long term trade deficits? Will there come a day when people crave a simpler life and start farming again?

31

Silly Notions about Actually Using Your Brain

Researchers are convinced that the average person uses only a fraction of their brain on any given day. If this is true, there should be an incredible intellectual resource just waiting to be tapped sitting in the burlap kennels around you. Then why is this resource so often ignored? How can this energy be drawn from for the good of the organization? With so much available brainpower, why is problem solving such a hot topic within most organizations? How can we learn to view "situations" as opportunities for improvement rather then with the negative stigma that normally is associated with the word problem?

There seems to be a general trend for employees within organizations to be moving towards Jack-of-all-Trades rather then specialists working together on common initiatives. We talk more about effective teamwork but seem to enjoy fewer results from it. The sport of throwing problems over the wall is as popular now as it ever was. We have the ability to generate huge amounts of information yet we can't seem to get to the point. More business is being conducted through impersonal channels rather then fostering bonds with the feeling that we're all in this together.

Are our leaders taking charge or are they blindly following an edict from above? Do they really know the business or did they come in after it was established long ago? Are we striving to be the biggest or the best or both? Do we believe them when they say things like this project will reduce the needed head count so that those individuals can be transferred to more value added activities?

Do we exercise our brains as much as we should? Are we as passionate about what we do as we should be? What would happen if someday someone were to invent an implantable brain meter that could track and record the amount of thought processes expended during the day? What if our compensation was based on the result? Would there need to be a more sensitive device for those in management?

Maybe we have come to rely too heavily on high technology and are missing out on some of the benefits of low technology. Will technology take our place in the work force with advancements in artificial intelligence? Just think about how much money the company could save on those lovely burlap kennels!

Not to fear for there is nothing that can compare to the creativity of the human mind. It has been said for many years that our only real limitation is our ability to imagine. The evidence of this being true is all around us!

32

Keeping the Pyramid Healthy

Without structure, no large group of people would come together for the greater good with much success. When a corporate pyramid is healthy, employees as well as the community at large will benefit in many ways. It is heartwarming to see how strong companies step up to the plate in order to support local charities as well as respond to natural and unnatural disasters around the world.

How healthy is the your pyramid?

In order to be effective, each manager should have between 5 and 10 employees reporting to them depending on the complexity of the work to be done. Any less and they'd be bored, any more and they would not be able to do their people justice. However, if you examine the typical large organization, these numbers can get way out of whack! It is very common for some managers to have no reports, while at the same time, others may have dozens. Wake up and do the math you executives, this can result in a very unhealthy pyramid if this trend continues for any length of time. It is amazing just how often people are given "management" titles when they have no direct reports. This is wrong and condescending to those rare good managers out there who are fighting the "good fight".

33

The Importance of Luck, Careful Planning, Timing, Creativity and Mouse Balls

Being in the right place at the right time with the right idea is and always will be of paramount importance. Careful planning, intelligence and hard work alone are not enough to ensure success in today's business climate. There are many tools at our disposal to help envision, plan and manage our work. We have high education, incredibly fast computers, brilliant business training and a host of new machines, materials and process technologies in our tool chests from which to draw from. Yet with out impeccable timing, positioning and most especially luck, failure is almost assured. Yet with perseverance and creativity on our side, fantastic opportunities for success are seemingly endless. Manage your companies by objectives but more importantly, reward your employees by results. No one can accurately predict what the future will hold so the most important thing is to keep trying and learning and be flexible enough to adapt to an ever-changing environment.

The original computer mouse designs included a weighted ball that came in contact with a desk top or mouse pad in order to send a signal of motion back to the computer. These balls included a steel core surrounded by an elastomer material to help provide enough traction so the ball would roll rather than slide across the surface. Since computers were being sold in large volumes, the company I was with at the time was very interested in producing these Mouse Balls. I was charged with coming up with a process for covering the steel ball in an efficient manor yet ensuring that it stayed perfectly centered within the elastomer coating. It took some work but I was very proud of the process and tooling that was developed. In the long run, my company could not compete with those with lower labor rates but the principles learned in developing this new process proved to be very useful in more lucrative opportunities that followed. As it turned out, computers now use a low power laser, which is more reliable and inexpensive than a mouse ball. Poor mice are ball-less now.

Change is inevitable and good. Learn to roll with the punches and keep your head up and you'll come out a winner in the long run.

34

Considering Some Alternatives

Your mid-life career crisis should hit about the time you become a senior jib. It's not that you won't be thankful for what you have; it's just that it will start to occur to you that there must be something better out there. Most likely, you will be beyond the point where professional sports are an option. You have been buying lottery tickets for years and that hasn't seemed to work out. You know you can't sing, dance or act worth a darn. Can sitting in a burlap kennel for another 15 years really be your true calling? Taking a chance on a new venture is a big risk with a mortgage to pay and kids in school. Why does it feel like your buying power has dwindled so much over the last decade? Picking up the newspaper or a magazine to read about the lucky entrepreneurs that have made it big only makes you feel like somehow you have really missed the boat. Why is it that these people are always high school dropouts and now they own huge homes in the Caribbean and Europe?

Well at least you have your health right? Or has the stress of the workplace finally started to take its toll on that too? No doubt all of those brownies you have been eating have caught up with your waistline!

Most likely you have done a little division jumping or tried a few other companies by now only to realize that the grass isn't that much greener.

It's not unusual to start engaging in a little creative daydreaming at this point in your career. Man, would it be fun to start up a little business doing something really fun if only you knew you could make a buck or two. Getting the chance to be your own boss seems like such an appealing concept after all these years!

One of my favorite fantasies has to do with the idea of working like mad until the age of say 45 and then taking a mid career retirement for 5 to 10 years before

90

returning to work. By working hard and saving diligently, early on, you would ensure that a financial nest egg would be initiated, for your "second" retirement, with many years for it to grow. By the time this "extended vacation" where to start, you would have the maturity to truly appreciate people, travel and experiencing other lands and cultures. At this age you would also still be in good enough physical condition so that there wouldn't be any limitations on the activities you could choose to engage in. There are just a few "little" details yet to be worked out in this scheme. Financing the time when not employed and finding a good job after such a long hiatus are among them.

The lucky few may escape life in the pyramid via a large inheritance or lottery winning. Although it seems like too many of these folks don't stay lucky for long! If they don't have major problems due to newly found wealth, their children often do.

If only there was another "legalized pyramid" where enough money could be raised, say something like writing a book?

Anyway, just about the time you envision yourself walking powdery white sand beaches in a tropical paradise, wham the telephone rings and your little 5-minute reverie is over as reality suddenly hits and you realize that you are indeed eternally trapped in The Corporate Zone!

978-0-595-37367-3
0-595-37367-4

Printed in the United States
80934LV00004B/585